£2

D1438838

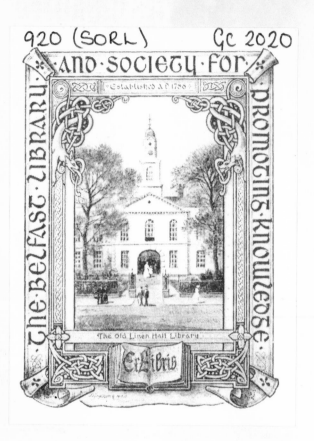

The Old Linen Hall Library

Charles Hamilton
SORLEY
A BIOGRAPHY

Charles Hamilton SORLEY

A Biography by
Jean Moorcroft Wilson

CECIL WOOLF · LONDON

First published 1985
©1985 Jean Moorcroft Wilson

Cecil Woolf Publishers, 1 Mornington Place, London NW1 7RP
Tel: 01-387 2394

British Library Cataloguing in Publication Data
Wilson, Jean Moorcroft
Charles Hamilton Sorley : a biography
1. Sorley, Charles Hamilton — Biography
2. Poets, English — 20th century — Biography
I. Title
821'.912   PR6037.072Z/
ISBN 0-900821-52-3

For Cecil

Contents

Illustrations

Acknowledgements: For their kind permission to reproduce photographs, the author and publishers are grateful to Miss Ursula Bickersteth (illustrations no. 1-17 inclusive, 21, 29 and 30); Brigadier Kaye (illustrations no. 18, 19 and 22); Marlborough College (illustrations no. 20, 24 and 26) and Rudolf Bakker (illustrations no. 23 and 25).

Endpapers: 'Sorley's Signpost', from a watercolour by his nephew, Julian Bickersteth, 1938. Courtesy of Miss Ursula Bickersteth.

Acknowledgements

It is sad that the person who has helped me most with this biography, Sorley's sister, Jean Bickersteth, died before it was published. However, I should like to thank her daughter, Ursula Bickersteth, very much indeed for continuing her valuable help, encouragement and advice. Other members of the family, particularly Mrs Kenneth Sorley, Mrs Iris Portal and Lord Balerno, were also very responsive to my needs.

My other main source of information came from Marlborough College, where the late Gerald Murray did all he could to encourage me. Laurence Ellis, the housemaster of C House whilst I was doing my research, provided me with a great deal of valuable information from the school archives and Beverley Heath provided excellent reproductions of school photographs. Mr Gidney, Mr Kempson, Colonel Awdrey, Pat Amps, Joseph Bain and Mrs O'Regan and her sons John and Michael were also exceedingly helpful as well as most hospitable.

For information about Sorley's King's College Choir School days I am grateful to both David Briggs and Dean Seriol Evans.

Finally, I am deeply indebted to Rudolf Bakker for the patience and skill he gave to copying old family photographs. Some of these, in their original form, were so faded and blurred that it would not have been practicable to reproduce them without such unstinted expert help.

J.M.W.

1
Childhood

Charles Hamilton Sorley was proud of his Scottish origin. Though he spent the greater part of his life in England, he never completely identified with the English. He was born in Aberdeen on 19 May 1895, the elder twin son of Professor William Ritchie Sorley and his wife, Janetta Colquhoun Smith. Both parents were, however, of Lowland rather than Highland descent, coming from the lands between the Tay and the Tweed. When Professor Sorley's brother applied for a family coat-of-arms, he was told that it was based on 'those of the Macdonalds, of which clan the Sorleys are believed to be sept'. More significantly perhaps both sides of Charles's family contained a number of writers and religious thinkers, as well as a plentiful share of strong-minded individualists.

Charles's paternal grandfather, William Sorley, was the son of Margaret Luke and James Sorley, headmaster and joint-proprietor of a school at Liverpool. Instead of following his father into teaching, William entered the Church and being of an independent nature 'came out' at the Disruption of the Church of Scotland in 1843, helping to found the Scottish Free Church. Of his reputed humour we have now no examples, but we do know that he was the author of at least two books— *Prospects and Perils of the Free Church* (1845) and *The Danger of an Uncertain Sound; or, Doctrine Defection Apprehended* (1847). Having started his ministry at Belhaven, East Lothian, he moved to Selkirk, where he married Anna Wilson Simpson Ritchie, had three children and shortly afterwards, in 1859, died. Left alone with three young children Anna Sorley coped remarkably well. The eldest daughter of William Hamilton Ritchie, described on the family coat-of-arms as a 'writer, banker and town-clerk of Dunbar', she had been used to a life of some comfort, bringing with her when she married her own silver and china. However as a young widow she was left with very little money and many problems. She continued to live at Selkirk for the children's primary education, then moved with them to Edinburgh. Since she died before any of her grandchildren were born, neither Charles, nor his twin-brother, nor sister remembered her, but a photograph taken in late life shows a woman of great determination and force of character, handsome even in old age.

Anna's eldest child, James, was almost certainly a victim of his family's sudden poverty, for he did not go on to complete his education at the University, as might have been expected. Instead he turned to business and, having inherited his father's keen mind, quickly succeeded, eventually becoming a director of the Pelican and British Empire Life Office in London. As a bachelor he felt the need of a settled home and invited his unmarried sister, Mary, to come and housekeep for him. She set up home for them, first at 32 Onslow Square, Kensington, later at 82 Onslow Gardens, and ran with great efficiency a butler, housemaid, parlourmaid and cook, until James's death, when she got rid of the butler. Charles enjoyed visiting his aunt and uncle in their London home and took full advantage of its comforts, as we shall see.

Mary Simpson Sorley, the only daughter of William and Anna, seems to have inherited her mother's determination and force of character. Having experienced poverty during her youth she was conscious of it all her life and when her own means improved helped many poor people, mainly old spinsters and widows with whom she could identify. So impressive were her efforts that when James died, rather than leaving money to a charity, he left her a large sum to dispense privately at her own discretion. Her nephew Charles was extremely fond of her and she returned his affection: 'they were great friends', his mother wrote. Charles admired Aunt Mary's forthrightness and she loved the way he was 'always trying, even as a small boy, to interest you'. He respected and shared her love of books, of which she had a good collection. She had had her own bookplate designed by an artist friend: 'Give me a nook and a book', it read, with a picture of a cosy armchair by a fire beneath it. Charles also admired the fine bookbinding she took up as a hobby and when he was at the Front in France sent her a copy of *The Imitation of Christ* in Flemish, with the hope that her 'professional opinion' would agree that it was 'quite a nice binding—for Belgium!' He teased her about her mistrust of doctors and her refusal to admit to any illness except a cold, in spite of which she lived to be ninety-six. Stubborn to the last she refused to leave London in the Second World War, even during the worst days of the blitz. 'What!' she is said to have exclaimed, 'and miss my Christmas shopping at Harrods?'

Mary's younger brother and Charles's father, William Ritchie Sorley, did not share her flamboyance. Born in 1855, he was only four when his father died, yet was much closer to him in character than to his mother. Reserved and solemn-looking, he often intimidated others at a first meeting, particularly children, as one niece still remembers. If they were bold enough to persevere with him, however, they discovered that he was really very gentle and had a remarkable sense of humour. His daughter Jean recalled that he enjoyed P.G. Wodehouse enormously, as well as a wide variety of more serious writers of all nationalities. As a young man he was very interested in religion and after taking his M.A. at Edinburgh University, devoted a further three years to the study of theology, with the intention of following his father into the Church. Though his conscience did not finally allow him to become a minister, he remained interested in theological matters throughout his life. While a student of moral science at Cambridge, Professor Sidgwick is said to have described William Sorley's inquiring attitude as that of 'a well-bred atheist listening to a sermon'. At the height of Sorley's distinguished career in moral philosophy, however, when he became Knightbridge Professor at King's College, Cambridge, Sidgwick himself told Sorley what a relief it was to have a *Christian* Philosopher to replace him.

Another feature William Ritchie Sorley inherited from his father, and was to pass on to his elder son, was his literary ability. During a very busy life of teaching and administration he published at least eight books and numerous papers, as well as contributing chapters to *The Cambridge History of English Literature*. He himself considered his best work to be *Moral Values and the Idea of God*, though he is perhaps better known for his *Ethics of Naturalism*.

Professor Sorley was above all a modest man, rarely discussing his work, even with his family. Comparing his own undoubted achievements with his son's he concluded: 'He will be remembered when I am a dead and forgotten scholar—there is in his poetry the *truth* I sought, and beauty such as I have never found'. Professor Sorley was on friendly terms with a number of famous men, including William Temple, later Archbishop of Canterbury. Though they had climbed mountains together, he did not expect Temple to remember him when they met at a Vice-Chancellor's party in Cambridge. 'Sorley,' he introduced himself, 'I don't suppose you'll remember me.' 'Remember you!' Temple replied in a loud and cheerful voice, 'don't I preach you up and down the country!' Charles was to inherit his father's modesty and to be preached in his turn.

Charles's mother's family, the Smiths, formed something of a contrast to the Sorleys. His maternal grandfather, George Smith, was a forceful man who had made his own way in the world. The son of a rope-maker and barber, who is said to have cut sailors' hair on the shores of Leith, George had risen to be headmaster of a school for Eurasian boys at Calcutta. This was not entirely surprising for George's father, like many Scots, combined a practical business ability with a deep respect for learning, which he passed on to his son. In addition the Scottish educational system of the time allowed a boy of promise from whatever social background to receive sound schooling and a university education if he wished. George Smith had not attended university, but he had become, in 1856 at the age of twenty-three, a Fellow and Examiner at Calcutta University and the following year had taken up the editorship of the *Calcutta Review*. He also edited another important Calcutta paper, *The Friend of India* (which later became *The Statesman*) and was Indian correspondent for *The Times* from 1860 to 1878. His forceful articles for the latter had, according to his daughter, 'focussed public attention on governmental abuses in India'. Like the Sorley family and his own father, who was something of a Shakespeare enthusiast, George Smith had literary leanings and wrote several books, among them a *Students' Geography of British India* and *Twelve Indian Statesmen*.

While in India George Smith had come under the influence of the well-known missionaries, Carey and Marshman, who had a number of interests at Serampore, near Calcutta, including a college and the publication of a daily newspaper. Though George Smith did not distinguish himself in theology, his eldest son, George Adam Smith, became a minister and an Old Testament scholar of some repute and another of his five sons also entered the Church. George Smith's reverence for religion and learning emerges very clearly in a story told by his granddaughter, who was taken by him as a small child to see Edinburgh University. 'This is where your father studied,' said George Smith, who admired his son-in-law William Sorley tremendously, 'and it's a great thing to be a *Christian* philosopher'. George Smith seems to have been a very lovable man: his granddaughter thought him 'a darling' and Charles, her brother, loved him dearly. Robert Frost, whose mother was Scottish, said Smith was his best friend in Edinburgh and frequently visited him there.

While still a young man in Calcutta George Smith had met and married Janet Colquhoun Adam, a 'woman of brains and character', according to her grandson, R.A. Butler. Lord Butler recalled that they had ten children 'who were sent home in batches to live with "the aunts" on the shores of the Firth of Forth'. However when the third son had joined his brothers in Scotland the eldest of them wrote solemnly to his father that 'two maiden aunts cannot manage boys' and the whole family, including his heavily pregnant mother, had had to return. Janet Colquhoun Adam died before any of her Sorley grand-children were born, though they knew and liked George Smith's second wife.

Lord Butler, whose mother, Annie, was the youngest daughter of George and Janet maintained that everything the Smith family did was original:

> Uncle Will kept a tame bear in his tea-garden in Assam and went all the way to Lahore to buy a tomb-stone for his wife's grave. Uncle Charles, Resident in Gilgat and known as 'Smith of Asia,' conducted an almost independent far-frontier policy to the great annoyance of Simla. Aunt Kate was baptized by a missionary called Mr. Jagadisha Battarcharjia. Uncle Dunlop was Private Secretary to Lord Minto and his diaries, edited by Martin Gilbert, have been published under the title *A Servant of India* (*The Art of the Possible*, pp. 4-5)

All these sagas were woven into the Butlers' childhood, and into the young Sorleys' too. Apart from the eccen-tricities of Uncles Will and Charles they took pride in the solid achievements of George Adam Smith, who became Principal of Aberdeen University. They knew and loved their Aunt Mary—'Mustard-with-Mutton-Minnie' they affectionately called her—and were proud of her gifts as a water-colourist. They also liked to hear Uncle James Dunlop recall his friendship with Kipling and relate some of Kipling's characters to people he had known in India. Only Aunt Isobel, who married a minister in the United Free Church, and Uncle Hunter, who himself became a clergyman, seem to have slipped out of the family legends.

Amongst this gifted family Charles's mother, Janetta Colquhoun Smith, stands out as a character in her own right. Many are the stories told of her. Born in India in 1869, she had met William Ritchie Sorley when her family moved to Edinburgh in the late seventies or early eighties, through her eldest brother George Adam Smith, a fellow-student of Sorley's at Edinburgh University. They married in 1889, when Janetta was twenty and William thirty-four. The marriage was a good one, perhaps because 'Will', as she fondly called him, was reserved enough to appreciate her outspoken, talkative gaiety. An attractive woman, she was thought by some a beauty, by some a buffoon, but by most an extremely gifted and likeable person.

Above all Janetta had a mind of her own at a time when it was very common for women to see the world through their husbands' eyes. She was well-educated for her day and would almost certainly have benefited from university, if it had been open to her. In spite of a puritanical upbringing her respect for good literature led her to reject the bowdlerised texts which were usually thought appropriate for children: 'She was too intelligent', her daughter Jean maintained, 'to be excessively evangelical or prudish'. When she read Shakespeare to the children, or they acted it together, it had to be the complete text. 'I remember a dear spinster friend once gave us Dickens-for-children books,' Jean wrote, '*Little*

David Copperfield, *Little Paul Dombey*, *Little Nicholas Nickleby*. Mother was furious; she was a fan of Dickens and wouldn't have him bowdlerised—"you must either read the real Dickens or not at all". She took him away.' Another sign of Janetta's intelligence was her attitude towards men, which was neither subservient, nor aggressive. Replying to Charles's description of Goethe's Gretchen as 'only an episode in Faust's career', her viewpoint is surprisingly balanced for her time:

> I am interested in your calling Gretchen's part of the story an 'episode'. I wonder, was it that to her? Women suffer for you, struggle for you, sin for you— spend themselves utterly—and, in the latter end, are apt to be labelled merely 'episodes'. I suppose it is 'the man's point of view', and perhaps a law of nature. I'm not complaining, only interested.

Unlike some of her friends she was not a suffragette, though she obviously did not think of herself as merely a wife and mother. She was an individual, whose sayings were long remembered in the family. When her daughter Jean went to Girton, Mrs Sorley said she liked it because it had a chapel *and* a swimming-pool and must therefore be 'both godly and healthy'. Some of her sayings seemed so 'naughty' to Jean as a girl that they often 'took your breath away'. She remembered that her mother, an accomplished pianist, was particularly good at burlesquing sentimental songs, such as Balfe's 'I shot an arrow into the air'. She chose 'the kind of song that curates might sing to vicars' daughters, who accompanied them, leering at them over the grand piano,' as Jean put it. The children enjoyed Mrs Sorley's piano-playing, especially when she got a book of school songs and they could bawl out the Eton boating song with her at the piano. They were also very fond of the old English and Scottish song books.

Janetta Sorley had her serious side. Possessed of a strong social conscience, like her sister-in-law Mary Sorley, she was responsible for setting up a district nurse in the area in which they lived. She also founded and ran a committee to arrange homes for deprived and orphaned children. Her introduction to Charles's *Letters* shows that she had some literary ability, which manifested itself later on in her book about Cambridge University, *King's Daughters* (1937). She was an unusual mixture of liveliness and reticence and in this Charles resembled her. His sister felt that he was very like their mother, especially in his way of talking.

Mrs Janetta Sorley was particularly delighted by the birth of her twin sons, Charles and Kenneth in 1895, for in 1892 she had lost a one-year-old son, Wilfred. Though somewhat consoled by the birth of a daughter, Jean, in 1893, it is fairly clear that she wanted another son to take the place of the one who had died. Jean's affection for her suggests that she did not allow this entirely to spoil her relationship with her daughter, but evidence suggests that she favoured sons. Jean did not remember being at all jealous of the twins, though she felt that being twins and both boys they were naturally closer to each other than to her. Nor did she recall any discrimination on her parents' part. As children all three played very happily together, building towns and railway stations with their toy bricks on the nursery floor, or exploring the grounds around their house.

A family anecdote told of Charles as a baby suggests that he was more advanced than usual in his development, though it is clearly dangerous to generalize about this. At the age of one Charles was taken with Jean and Kenneth to visit an Aberdeen neighbour famous for her oat-cakes. 'Eh, yon Chairlie's wise!' she told Mrs Sorley afterwards. 'He came in, an' he looks roon, gaes up to the table an' sits doon an' opens his mooth an' says "Cake!"' Charles did not normally behave in a partic-

ularly precocious way, however. As a child and even as
a young woman, Jean did not think of him as 'anything
special' and certainly did not realize that he wrote as
much poetry as he did later on. She remembered him as
a happy, well-adjusted child. Her clearest memories of
Kenneth were that he had croup and was 'supposed to
be delicate'; he did not play many games and, when he
did, 'he held his bat or racket rather sloppily, unlike
Charles who always stood up very straight'. As very
small boys, she recalls, Charles was the 'solemn, solid
one', Kenneth the more frisky, but Charles grew gayer
as he developed and loved a joke. Like his father he was
particularly fond of word-play and one of Jean's most
vivid childhood memories concerns one of Charles's puns.
They were at the seaside with a family called the Conways
and when their little girl, Ruth, ran shivering away from
the icy North Sea, Charles shouted to Jean and Kenneth
scornfully and with glee 'Ruth Conway's gone 'way!'
Charles was undoubtedly far more confident than his
rather timid twin and Jean felt it unfortunate that
Kenneth should have had such a gifted brother, with
whom he was invariably contrasted.

Kenneth himself seems to have had understandably
mixed feelings about Charles. On the one hand he was
very close to him and felt desolate when they were
eventually sent to different schools. On the other he
could not conceal a certain resentment against Charles
for the effortless ease with which he succeeded in almost
everything he did. Replying to an enquiry about his
brother's poetry after his death, he burst out: 'Charles,
Charles, Charles; it's always Charles!' He found Charles's
work 'superficial', he said in later life. And yet it is
likely that their mother was right when she wrote: 'The
boys were alike in the deep love and understanding they
had for each other'. She was certainly right to say that
they had 'great independence of ideas and outlook and
were—for twins—remarkably different in nature and

appearance'. Kenneth was a highly nervous, timid child, fearful even of his own father who seemed to him a somewhat forbidding figure with his reserved and at times brusque manner. Charles, who was quite bold with Professor Sorley, even daring to interrupt him at his work, got on very well with him. Kenneth seems to have been much closer to his mother, who was rather protective towards him. This was partly because of his delicate health, but partly because she identified with Kenneth, as she explained to a friend:

> I feel much touched by what you tell me of your brother's conviction that he was a failure for *I know* in myself what such a knowledge means and how hard it is to think otherwise. Charlie who had none of the sense of it himself yet had an amazing sympathy and discernment of it in others, partly because he loved and understood so well Kenneth who is like me in that. What seemed failure, the unaccomplishment of fruition always attracted Charlie; success and self-assurance he left alone.

Looking back on a healthy uncomplicated childhood Charles reflected: 'Health—and I don't know what ill-health is invites you so much to smooth and shallow ways'. He had an almost apologetic attitude towards those less fortunate: 'I often feel terribly unworthy and untried', he wrote in 1915, 'in that life has given me no troubles or difficulties at home, such as alone strengthen a man'. And on more than one occasion he defended the failures, perhaps with Kenneth in mind: 'The common unattractive specimen whose life is confined to "second hour"[1] or Third—,[2] who is "supered"[3] as soon as pos-

[1] *'second hour'* i.e. an extra hour of prep.

[2] *'Third'* i.e. the third eleven, or fifteen.

[3] *'supered'* i.e. short for 'superannuated', which in this context means being asked to leave school early.

sible', he wrote to a friend, 'and who is called a "worm" because he is merely physically and intellectually not so pushing as the majority, generally does far more to justify any bump of conceit he may nourish in secret than the average successful specimen with a tie for every day in the week'.[1] Though more gifted than Kenneth in almost everything but musical ability, Charles cared greatly about his brother's opinion, especially when on one occasion Kenneth accused him of conceit—'What conceited thing have I done?' he pleaded, very upset. But usually Charles was in control and, like his mother, rather protective towards his slower twin.

Charles's attitude towards his mother was less complex—affectionate and teasing in turn, but always very loving. When she tried to badger him into showing her his poems in his teens, he at first refused, but a few weeks later started to send batches of them to her, often on her birthday, which he faithfully remembered. Though he hated having his photograph taken, he did so for her sake occasionally—as 'a kind of appeasement'. He wrote to her frequently once he had left home and enjoyed her letters to him 'better than all the books you send', he told her.

All in all the Sorleys were a happy family. In 1896, one year after the twins' birth and two years after Professor Sorley's appointment as Regius Professor of Moral Philosophy at Aberdeen University, they moved from a quite ordinary house in Don Street to Powis House, a fine Adam mansion. Powis House had been left to a young man called 'Jackie Burnett of Powis', who was not allowed to occupy the house till he was twenty-five, so the Sorleys had been fortunate enough to rent it at a price they could afford. Situated high above Old Aberdeen, with a marvellous view of King's College and

---

[1] *tie for every day of the week*' i.e. different ties were awarded for different achievements, so that the more successful you were the greater choice of ties you had to wear.

the North Sea it was, as Mrs Sorley wrote, 'a fine windy place and a good natural nursery for children'. While Professor Sorley prepared lectures in his study or held discussions of the Philosophical Club, which he had started to encourage his students with more informal contact, the children played in the surrounding fields, often inventing stories about the animals they saw there.

Sometimes they were taken by their nanny to visit her parents' farm at Sheilhill, near Peterhead, where they learnt to plant potatoes and other 'barn-door wisdom'. Mrs Sorley had been very fortunate in her choice of nanny, for all three children adored Jean Porter. Though not demonstrative she returned their deep affection and remained in the family till her retirement. Charles, of whom she was especially proud, wrote to her from France years after he had left her care. Thanking her for a present of cigarettes, he asked: 'Are you going to Scotland at all this summer? If so tell them there that there's a farm just like Sheilhill behind our trenches—same little garden and everything—but smashed alas to ruins'. Jean Porter had had a tough upbringing by a severe father on the remote Highland farm and was herself a great disciplinarian. She did not hesitate to smack her charges if they disobeyed her strict rules, particularly ones related to cleanliness and tidiness. Being highly efficient in practical matters, she expected the same standard of the young Sorleys. Nevertheless she had the imagination to realise that children needed more than simply to be kept clean and obedient, so on the cook's day off she would take Jean, Kenneth and Charles into the kitchen and let them make drop-scones with her—in the shape of their own initials. (She was very tactful with the kitchen staff, Jean remembered, unlike many nannies, and was therefore allowed to take over the kitchen on such occasions.)

Nanny Porter also contributed to the children's education. As a Scotswoman she was almost certainly better educated than her English counterpart would have been and she read aloud to the Sorleys while they were still too young to read for themselves. Being a devout Presbyterian, she tended to concentrate on religious books, wanting to give her charges a solid religious grounding.

Not surprisingly perhaps the Sorley children were more excited by the much wider variety of books read to them by their mother. There were the usual children's books—Hans Andersen, Grimm's Fairy Tales, Andrew Lang's Blue and Pink Fairy books and the Alice stories, which they enjoyed most of the classics. Then there was a series of little pink-paper-covered works called *Books for the Bairns* which included simplified versions of *Robinson Crusoe* and *Gulliver's Travels*, and occasionally *The Boys Own Paper*. They were particularly excited by the children's magazine *Little Folks*, which was edited by Bella Sidney Woolf and contained a long serial by her, *All in a Castle Fair*. Inspired by the adventures of Archie, Lesley and Sydney and the romantic scenery of a Scott-like landscape similar to their own surroundings, the young Sorleys started to invent their own saga, rather like the young Brontës. Since the twins were well under five, however, the episodes were not committed to paper, but they were related to Mrs Sorley. She remembered that it centred around an imaginary kingdom 'up the line', connected by a vast railway system. This was based on their local station, Kitty Brewster, where they had once seen Queen Victoria changing trains for Balmoral! It amused their mother to learn that one of the rules of her children's kingdom was 'that all officials must cross the line by the bridges only, while passengers and others might do as they pleased'. In Charles's case at least, it was an early sign of his questioning of authority, which continued throughout his life. The invention of the saga itself is a very early indication of his fertile imagination and literary inclinations.

A further encouragement to literary creation came from Professor Sorley, who was always inventing little verses for his children, one of which has survived from this period. It was written to accompany a present of a hobby-horse for Christmas:

ACROSTIC

HE RAN AS FAST AS HE WAS ABLE
BUT NEVER LEFT HIS LITTLE STABLE

Hurrah	Often longed for, long expected Here at last the gee-gee stands, Look and when you've well inspected Little trio clap your hands.
Oh No	Never sit him with unkind legs, Never pull his bridle tight, Never kick his nose or hind legs, Never put him in a fright.
Brother	Think of him as more than wooden With like feelings to your own; Love him now as if he couldn' 'T more akin to you have grown.
Boys	Slick your legs across the saddle, Let the charger gaily go, You must sit the beast astraddle, Leave the pommel to Jeano.
Yule	And may this best of Christmas toys Ever carry happy faces; Happy girl and happy boys Showing all the Christmas graces.

Powis House, Aberdeen, Christmas, 1898.　　*W.R.S.*

It is unlikely that Charles started to write his own verse in Aberdeen, since he was only five when the family left, but the seeds were undoubtedly sown there. It is not until the Sorleys moved to Cambridge at the turn of the century that we have evidence of him beginning his literary career in earnest.

2
King's College Choir School

As the twentieth century dawned and young under-graduates like Lytton Strachey, Leonard Woolf, Thoby Stephen and Clive Bell were gathering at Cambridge to form the embryo of Bloomsbury, Professor Sorley was joining their mentors, Russell, Moore, McTaggart and Whitehead in the faculty of Moral Science. For in 1900 Professor Sorley had succeeded Sidgwick as Knightbridge Professor of Moral Philosophy and shortly afterwards became a fellow of King's. He already knew Bertrand Russell and George Moore well, since he had been at Trinity on a postgraduate scholarship in the 1880s. Yet though as Quentin Bell argues, 'Bloomsbury was begotten in Cambridge at the beginning of the century', Professor Sorley and his family were almost completely ignorant of the ferment in their midst. So much so that when Bertrand Russell and G.E. Moore came to lunch with the Sorleys on occasions, all Jean Sorley could remember was that she had disliked Russell 'because he was so ugly'! She got on well with Moore, but only because he was 'very keen on the bumping races, as we were, and used to run down the tow-path cheering the first Trinity boat. So one felt he was a human being'. She recalled that her mother, when she heard of Bloomsbury's views and doings later on, 'thoroughly disapproved of them and wouldn't have anything to do with them, even though one of them, a Stephen, was nephew to Sir Harry Stephen whom my father had been at college with'. Mrs Sorley did not know Maynard Keynes as an undergraduate, but she disliked his mother, whom she thought 'bossy'. Professor Sorley was a close friend of Keynes's father, with whom he played golf, but he had no real contact with Maynard, nor any awareness of his role in the formation of Bloomsbury.

For Professor and Mrs Sorley Cambridge did not mean meetings of the Apostles' Society, with its frank discussions of such problems as censorship and relations between the sexes, nor did it mean thrilling meetings at midnight, which ended at dawn with wild poetry recitations. For the Sorleys Cambridge meant a continuation of the gentle social intercourse they had known in Aberdeen, a round of calls, 'At Homes', luncheons, teas and dinner-parties. Their guests were mainly Cambridge dons and their wives, apart from Sunday lunch when they entertained Professor Sorley's final-year students. On Sunday mornings there was church for the whole family—King's College Chapel for the parents and the Children's Service at Trinity Church for the young Sorleys. (Charles was very good at answering the vicar's questions there, Jean recalled.) Yet the Sorleys, being Scottish, were possibly a little freer of social pressures than most English families of similar standing. They were certainly enlightened for their time. Professor Sorley had a number of foreign students, mostly Indians, and Jean remembered her parents telling the children that they were of the same race as themselves and *not* to be looked down on.

Instead the Sorley children looked down on the English, who could not, to their amazement, pronounce their '*h*s' or '*r*s'! Both parents spoke with a perceptible Scots accent, which the children lost as they grew up, though they continued to use Scots idioms. The move to Cambridge at such an impressionable age must have heightened their sense of being Scottish and, therefore, different. Charles often referred to what he jokingly called his 'Scotchness': 'Excuse this half-sheet,' he wrote to a friend. 'It's not my Scotchness, really, only the fact that it's all the notepaper I've left'. Yet he was undoubtedly proud of his ancestry. When he saw the Irish players performing Yeats's *Cathleen Ni Houlihan* and Synge's *The Playboy of the Western World*, he wrote to his father: 'They are both great plays of their kind: bringing home to me, and making me glad of, my Celtic origin'.

In spite of having to leave their beloved Scotland, Charles, Kenneth and Jean were very excited by the move. For one thing it meant a long journey and an overnight stay with a Presbyterian friend of their parents in Glasgow on the way. It also meant a new home to explore when they reached Cambridge. St Giles, the house their parents chose as a temporary expedient, was not nearly as elegant as Powis, but it was spacious and had a large garden for them to play in. The twins were put together on the second and highest floor in a room which overlooked Magdalene College and the Cam. It was almost certainly with this view in mind that Charles was later to write:

I know that there is beauty where the low streams run,
And the weeping of the willows and the big sunk sun

Despite such changes, there was some continuity in the children's lives at Cambridge. Nanny Porter had come with them and was to remain another five or six years before leaving to help their Aunt Annie (Butler) with her children in India. Mrs Sorley continued to read to them, progressing now to Scott's *Quentin Durward*, *The Monastery*, *The Abbot*, *Ivanhoe* and some of the ballads, perhaps out of nostalgia for her home country. She also organised family readings of Shakespeare's plays, among them *The Merchant of Venice*, *A Midsummer Night's Dream* and *The Two Gentlemen of Verona*. Charles, who was only five when they started, enjoyed these readings greatly—'even so [they] were apt to end in tears'. They left him with a deep appreciation of Shakespeare which increased as he matured. 'I can't read Shakespeare to myself,' he wrote to his parents years after the family readings had ceased; 'but it is a different thing for a "group" to read it aloud, as we used to do'.

More lightheartedly there were family games. For the children, beside their bricks, there were toy soldiers and, later on, cricket in the garden, though that tended to be destructive of flowers. Croquet was considered much less dangerous and there are several photographs of the whole Sorley family enjoying a game together. Indoors there were dominoes, draughts, solitaire, spillikins, lexicon and, eventually, chess. Professor Sorley was a keen card player and taught them various kinds of Patience, until they were ready for whist and bridge.

Every summer there were family holidays. In the early 1900s as very young children they went to stay at an inn in the East Yorkshire village of Ellerby. The two old sisters who ran it were excellent cooks and Charles, who loved good food, remembered as one of the 'outstandingly admirable meals' of his life 'one in Yorkshire, in an inn upon the moors, with a fire of logs and ale and tea and every sort of Yorkshire bakery'. His hostesses returned his admiration: 'There goes Charlie, aye bright and brave', one of them was heard to remark at the end of a holiday. The children were allowed to help a girl called Ada milk the cows and afterwards they would walk across the moors with their parents to the nearby sea. Jean slept with Nanny in a huge feather-bed, while Charles shared another with Kenneth. There were at least two holidays spent with cousins which the children enjoyed. One was with their Butler cousins at Tintagel. Iris Portal (née Butler) remembers how they all took the train to Camelford, then transferred to a wagonette, which drove them to their communal boarding-house. They went for long picnics together, she recalls, with a donkey called Polly to carry the food. Except for her father's irritation at the state in which Kenneth left the bathroom, the holiday seems to have been a great success, particularly some outings to the beautiful Bosinhay Bay. Another enjoyable summer was spent with Aunt Kate's children, the Townsends, who took a house next to the Sorleys at Dunwich, Suffolk in 1906. One of the excitements of that particular holiday was hearing Nanny addressing the Townsends' French nanny in her own language: 'Mar-r-ie, ouvr-r-ez la por-r-te,' Jean remembered her saying. The Sorleys' most curious holiday was spent at Blair Atholl in 1907, when they lodged at the stationmaster's house. Since all trains had to stop there (a condition on which the Duke had allowed the railway to be built through his land) the Sorleys would sometimes see their friends on the London-Inverness train from their room overlooking the station. The whole family would then rush down to talk to them on the platform. They returned to Scotland the following year to visit their parents' close friends, the Harrowers. John Harrower was Professor of Greek at Aberdeen University and his wife was the only daughter of Sir William Geddes, Principal of the University. They lived in a staff house, which was called, for obvious reasons, The Greek Manse and there are numerous photographs of the Sorleys taken there. The Harrowers had no children and, while the adults talked at meal-times, the young Sorleys had to sit in silence. They entertained themselves secretly, however, by laying bets in advance as to who would come off best in the discussions and were often convulsed with laughter as they waited for the results.

Life was not all play at Cambridge. For the twins now began their education in earnest. At first they were taught at home by their mother, who undoubtedly made learning exciting, particularly literature. Mrs Sorley herself has told us what she taught them:

Their education, besides the acquisition of an angular handwriting, consisted chiefly in singing and marching games in French and English, history stories and fairy stories, reading aloud from the Bible and the *Pilgrim's Progress*, but especially in learning by heart any amount of poetry—ballads and passages of Shakespeare,

Walter Scott, Macaulay, and Blake.

Most of their poetry came from a popular collection called *Lyra Heroica*. Charles joked about its somewhat jingoistic nature later on, but it is clear that it helped shape his own poetic gifts by giving him a solid grounding in traditional English verse. Though Mrs Sorley did not venture to teach the twins classical languages, they must have known a little of them, for Kenneth's nickname was Paede, Greek for child. Charles nicknamed himself Little Wingay, after one of his literary heroes.

When the boys were nine Mrs Sorley had, regretfully, to send them to school. King's College Choir School was the natural choice. Not only was it one of the two best preparatory schools in Cambridge, but it was also near enough for the twins to attend as day-boys, which pleased their mother greatly. At King's College Choir School day-boys were not, as at most good prep. schools, in the minority; there were between twenty and thirty of them, while the boarders numbered the sixteen choristers and a dozen other boys. Nor were the day-boys looked down on; on the contrary, being sons of Cambridge dons, they were respected and largely responsible for the school's high educational achievements. Charles's own particular friend at school, Arthur Bethune-Baker, was a don's son and so too were the three Duff brothers who attended at the same time. Day-boys, boarders and choristers alike shared most of the timetable. The day-boys were naturally not expected to attend 'early school' before breakfast and only the choristers were given frequent choir practices, but everyone had to be in King's College Chapel on Sunday mornings, whether they could sing or not. Charles, who took after his father not his mother in this respect, had no ear for music, though he loved it and joined in lustily with the singing in chapel. His mother had taught him to enjoy singing from an early age, though she failed to persuade him to persevere

29

with the piano. Charles regretted his lack of musical ability: 'I should be quite happy,' he wrote to his mother in his teens, 'if only I could sing—were it never so little'. Kenneth, on the other hand, took after his mother in his good ear for music and skill at the piano.

The twins were more equal in their academic achievements, at least to begin with. Considering Charles's performance later on it is surprising to find how poorly he did at school in his first three years. He was frequently next to bottom in Greek, Latin and Maths, with Kenneth usually bottom, except in French, where their positions were reversed. It was not until English became accepted as a respectable academic subject, worthy of inclusion in the timetable, that Charles began to draw ahead of Kenneth. At its introduction in the summer term of 1907, Charles came fourth in English, while Kenneth came thirteenth at the bottom of the list. In the following term Charles came top in English, though still quite near the bottom in Latin, Greek, Maths and French. His general performance improved noticeably in his last two terms, when he was again top in English, winning a prize for the subject and a scholarship to a good public school in his final term, Summer 1908. Meantime Kenneth's results grew if anything worse and the gap which had previously been felt mainly in their personal confidence, widened considerably. Kenneth had from the beginning of school shown his usual timidity with boys and masters alike, while Charles was confident and popular with both. Dean Seriol Evans, who was at school with the twins clearly recalls the contrast between them. Kenneth he thought 'rather slow and very quiet', Charles he found 'much brighter', though also rather quiet; 'he had confidence in his own ability but was not arrogant or overbearing. He never pushed himself forward and seemed not to have much ambition. He was always very pleasant and good-tempered, always smiling'.

There is one story about Charles at King's College

Choir School which suggests a rather different side to his nature. During a history lesson one day the master happened to mention Adam Smith, author of *The Wealth of Nations*. Charles became very excited and tried to interrupt·but was ignored. Refusing to be squashed he finally burst out: 'Please, sir, Adam Smith was our great-grandfather!' This did not seem to impress the master, who probably thought he was showing off. When Mrs Sorley told Charles that his Smith great-grandfather had been a barber in Leith, rather than a famous economist, and that he must apologise, he rebelled. The master's response had not been that of a gentleman, he told Kenneth, and he did not therefore deserve an apology.

E.M.S. Wood, another contemporary of Charles at the Choir School, has one quite vivid memory of him there:

> It must have been a wet morning for it was during 'break', 11.30 to 12, and we were all confined, something of a crowd, in the big schoolroom instead of rushing about noisily outside. I can see Charles Sorley now, totally lost in his own thoughts, pacing slowly up and down the room regardless of the mob around him, dabbing his nose with his bunched up handkerchief, just a personal habit, I think, not provoked by a cold (Letter from E.M.S. Wood to A. Ernest Owen, 22 January 1978)

It is interesting that all who remember Charles at prep. school agree that, though usually very out-going, there were times when he was withdrawn and introspective. He retired into a world of his own, perhaps planning another of the long epic poems he had begun to write even before starting school. Most of these epics were based on Scott or Macaulay, whom his mother had taught him to love. His sister remembered one he composed about the battle of Killiekrankie and another about Lord Dundee, neither of which has survived. Nor has the poem he wrote in the manner of 'Hiawatha', which Mrs

Sorley had read to her children at an early age. Charles continued to write at King's College Choir School, to the exclusion of other things, as his mother relates:

> It is sad to have to record that well-meant efforts to interest [the twins] in natural history failed completely, nor did they ever have much inclination to collect stamps, play with bottles, or maim themselves with tools. But they were eager to write down whatever came into their heads or seemed to them worth remembering and telling about.

There were few opportunities for Charles to show his literary abilities at school to begin with. As we have seen neither English Literature nor Language was put on the timetable until his last years there and the school magazine, also started in his final years, contained only a few poems, all written by masters or Old Boys. Dean Evans's sole memory of his literary potential is the way in which he answered questions in class 'in a rather mature manner—he was more articulate than the majority of boys and had more idea of the use of language'.

In 1905, during Charles's second year at the Choir School, T.C. Weatherhead succeeded Mr Benham as headmaster. Mr Benham and his unmarried sister had run the school on comfortable but not very ambitious lines. A King's Scholar at Eton, Weatherhead was a good classicist and after a year or two of his teaching the boys began to win scholarships in classics to most of the major public schools.

Latin and Greek were of course the main subjects on the curriculum, the senior boys being taught by Weatherhead, the younger by an impecunious scholar from King's. Then there were Maths, ranging from simple arithmetic for the small boys to the more complex algebra and geometry for the older. Charles, as we have seen, never really shone at maths. Years later, when forced to take a maths paper for an important scholarship, he showed his scorn for the subject. 'If X started walking from ditto etc etc how far is it from Cambridge to Ely?' one of the questions ran. 'Seventeen miles,' Charles answered simply: 'I've bicycled it often'. The rest of the curriculum was divided among French, History, Geography and Divinity, which was taught by King's College chaplain, F.E. Hutchinson. Charles had been brought up on the Bible and knew it well. He was always ready to answer questions about the meaning of Alpha and Omega and other puzzles. It is no surprise to find frequent biblical references in his poetry later on.

Lessons took up most of the morning and part of the early evening, but the afternoons were reserved for games. Weatherhead, beside being a scholar, was also a fine athlete, having played football for both the Corinthians and the Casuals, the best amateur clubs of the day, and cricket for the Eton Ramblers. He encouraged the boys to enjoy football and cricket themselves, often sitting beside them at a school match and making up impromptu verses on the game. Matches were reserved for Saturday afternoons, school games for weekdays. Charles was not outstanding at either cricket or football and never played in a school team. Dean Evans relates this to a lack of ambition in him. It is perhaps arguable that without a strong sense of competition it is impossible to excel at team games. Charles participated willingly, however, and seems to have enjoyed them, as he enjoyed almost everything. His mother records that 'the beginning of school-life . . . meant nothing but satisfaction and happy anticipation to Charlie'. She tells how sad he was when he learnt in the spring of 1905 that scarlet fever would mean six weeks' separation from school and from Kenneth: 'No I haven't got a pain,' he explained to her when she found him crying after the news, 'but I can't help it when I think of the future'. This was almost the only occasion she remembered him being depressed.

Kenneth, on the other hand, was rather unhappy at prep. school. His natural slowness was accentuated by

Charles's quickness and everyone noticed it. Weatherhead, who had a sharp tongue and was possibly not as patient as he might have been, called Kenneth 'Brer Rabbit', implying that he was only Charles's timid little brother, not a person in his own right. He even published a verse in the school magazine the term Kenneth left for Westminster, entitled 'Brer Rabbit', which clearly reveals his scorn for him:

Our Brer Rabbit chewed a chew,
Nibbled nibbles, blinked and crew,
'Passed to Westminster!' (He thought the *house* was meant).

But his pride began to cool
When they packed him off to *school*!
Little Brer 'lay low' and had to be content.

Charles was as annoyed as Kenneth at the verse, in spite of a far more favourable one about himself, which appeared in the same issue entitled 'The Canny Gael':

Men have whispered it was brain
Helped the Canny Gael to gain
Such a Lucrative-Emolument-and-all.
But—to fling away pretence,
In the strictest confidence—
'Twas that fetching little Aberdonian drawl.

While the twins were coping with life at King's College Choir School, their sister was attending a small Dame School locally. Jean, who shared her brothers' interest in writing, offered to organise the school magazine with two or three friends. They each wrote something for it themselves and passed it on. Brothers or sisters with any talent were asked to contribute. Among other efforts Charles offered the following verses:

The Tempest

The tempest is coming,
The sky is so dark,

The bee has stopped humming
And down flies the lark.

The clouds are all uttering
Strange words in the sky;
They are growling and muttering
As if they would die.

Some forked lightning passes
And lights up the place,
The plains and the grasses,
A glorious space.

It is like a story
The light in the sky:
A moment of glory
And when it will die.

The rain is beginning,
The sky is so dark,
The bird has stopped singing
And down flies the lark.

Though this is obviously the work of a child, there are parts of it which anticipate Charles's later poetic achievements. In choosing the elemental, even violent aspects of nature, he prepares the way for many other poems about wind, rain and storm, which seem to stir him more deeply than the gentler features of nature. The detail here, as in later poems, is well observed: 'The tempest is coming . . . And down flies the lark'. The simple stanza form, the rhythm and the rhyme are all quite skilfully handled for a ten-year-old and the poem is neatly rounded off by a repetition, with variations, of the opening verse. It is in the imagery that his originality shows itself most clearly. The clouds 'uttering/Strange words in the sky . . . As if they would die' is an unusual notion. So too is the comparison of the lightning to a story: 'A moment of glory/And then it will die'. Altogether the poem shows promise. Charles's poetic career had begun.

3
Marlborough, 1908-1909

Charles was a pioneer in his choice of a public school, for his family had no previous experience or tradition to guide them. Characteristically he settled the question for himself by winning an open scholarship to Marlborough in 1908. Since only seven a year were awarded his parents were justifiably proud of him, but even more concerned about Kenneth. They had been upset by Weatherhead's discrimination between the twins and decided to prevent any further unfavourable comparisons by sending Kenneth to another school. He went to Westminster, then when he proved unhappy there, to a quiet local Methodist school, the Leyes.

So in September 1908, at the age of thirteen, Charles set off without his twin for Marlborough. However, there was all the novelty of a long journey and a new place to distract him. First he took the train from Cambridge to King's Cross, then a short trip along Euston and Marylebone Roads to Paddington, where he caught the 'special' to Marlborough. Arriving at the small country station, he had to descend the hill and pass through the long, broad High Street, with its mixture of little red-roofed houses, elegant Georgian façades and plentiful teashops, tuckshops and hotels, all designed to attract college custom. Once at the school gates he was taken over by the Porter, Sheppard, who passed him on to the stout college lamp-lighter, Green (known irreverently as 'Bloater Bill') to be led to 'A' House, for Junior boys. 'A' House was of fairly recent construction and rather resembled a prison in its square bleakness, but as Sorley crossed the school grounds to reach it, he saw through the trees a much older, more gracious building of mellow red brick. This, he learnt afterwards, had been built as a country house for the Seymours on the site of a Norman motte castle, and had later been turned into the Castle Inn, which flourished until coaches were forced off the Bath road by the extension of the Great Western Railway in the 1840s. Around this historic building had grown up over centuries similar buildings and when the Inn was converted to a school in 1843, a large schoolroom and three adjoining classrooms had been added. As the number of boys increased other new buildings sprang up, notably the Chapel at the end of the century.

Though the main buildings were old, the school itself was relatively new. It had been started in 1843 by the Reverend Charles Plater, who felt that there was a need for a good public school which the clergy could afford. The fees were therefore very low, but so unfortunately were the standards. Living conditions were so harsh and food so inadequate that less than ten years after opening the boys nearly wrecked the school in protest, smashing windows and furniture then setting fire to their rooms. It was a turning point in Marlborough's history, for the Reverend G.E. Cotton, who was brought in to restore order in 1852, quickly improved the school's performance and reputation, thus saving it from financial ruin. He brought with him from Rugby several new masters and began to run Marlborough on Dr Arnold's lines. In a letter to parents in 1853 he emphasised the importance of 'healthy and manly games' (as opposed to the bird-watching popular with earlier Marlburians!) and the need to establish house libraries. He was among the first to see that not all boys were intended for 'an academical career' and proposed to introduce not only modern languages and science but also crafts such as carpentry.

By the time Sorley arrived in 1908 most of these changes had been long established. Indeed under Frank Fletcher, the third assistant master from Rugby to rule Marlborough, the Modern side was greatly encouraged. The boys were still predominantly sons of clergymen and the fees were still low, at £105 a year (£30 of which in

Sorley's case was covered by his scholarship). But the number of boys had risen from the original 200 to nearly 650 and the assistant masters from 5 to 36. Marlborough had also by this time formed its traditions and like most public schools it had certain rituals for new boys, as Sorley found out. One trial new 'bugs' had to endure took place in dormitory each Saturday night. There were usually pairs of rings hanging from the beams and new boys were forced to carry out an excrutiating exercise called 'pull-through'. If they failed, which they often did through panic, they were given three strokes—in pyjamas! Another trial on Saturday nights were dormitory concerts in which everyone, except the captains, had to sing—an extremely painful experience if, like Sorley, you had no voice. However, he never complained of any of these ordeals. What he did remember vividly six years afterwards was that he was 'mocked' on arrival. This was almost certainly because, as a scholar, he entered the school quite high up. Beverley Nichols, who came to Marlborough four years later than Sorley, describes the treatment given to clever new boys in his autobiographical novel, *Prelude*:

> The new boys clustered together in awe on the outside of the groups, utterly disregarded by the rest of their fellows—except now and then to be asked a question as to how on earth they managed to get up so high right at the beginning, and generally to receive the impression that they had done a rather contemptible thing in writing a good entrance exam. (*Prelude*, 1920, p. 187)

Louis MacNeice is more explicit about the miseries of being a new boy at Marlborough:

> Physical discomfort and futile ritual—those were the first things I noticed. I entered a junior house where boys of about fourteen lived for a year or so to be

hardened before they moved on. Boys of that age being especially sadistic, life in the junior houses was more uncomfortable than the supposedly more frightening life we moved on to. The house itself looked like a prison, a great square building of ugly brick, with a huge well down the centre surrounded by railed-in landings; you could look up from the basement, see the prisoners listlessly parading on every floor, their shrill voices echoing metallic, the air sombre and stale, steaming in the morning from the bathrooms and dense in the afternoons with frying fat. There were often one or two little boys trudging down and up the stairs from the ground floor to the basement, turning automatically at the bottom step or the top, just down and up, down and up; these boys were doing 'Basements'—a punishment inflicted on them by boys one term or more their seniors. (*The Strings Are False*, p. 80)

As Beverley Nichols records 'turfing down basement' was a custom peculiar to A House and the penalty for refusal was 'Library', which meant 'three strokes of the cane in a barn-like room, surrounded by yelling youths'. Some boys remembered A House for its distinctive smell of sweaty socks and boiled cabbage, but Nichols remembers it for its noise:

There must have been something magic about [A House] . . . because a boy would wander across Court towards it looking entirely quiet and decorous, and as soon as he set his foot in the stone porch a piercing shriek would rise from his lips and often continue, with short breaks, for a period of several hours.

Attempting to control this pandemonium in A House were two housemasters, reigning over 'Upper' and 'Lower Landing' respectively. Sorley was fortunate enough to get C.A. Emery, who remained his housemaster, with a short break for eleven out of Sorley's sixteen terms at the school. The son of the Archdeacon of Ely, Emery had himself been at Marlborough as a boy and, after getting a first at Cambridge, had been teaching there nine years when Sorley arrived. He was then thirty-two and an experienced teacher and housemaster—'a charmer' is how one of his pupils described him. His main interest was music, though it was not his subject, and he helped to revise the Marlborough Hymn Book during his time there. Emery grew to have 'the warmest affection and regard' for Sorley he told his mother, and to admire 'his sterling character'.

The boys' less intellectual needs were cared for in A House by a 'Dame', who unpacked their luggage, looked after their laundry and generally mothered them. At least this was so in the case of Mrs Booth, who welcomed Sorley to A House in September 1908. For their meals they were sent to the large rather bleak Hall, where according to Louis MacNeice the older boys took advantage of their newness:

For the first few weeks I got very little to eat because I did not understand the custom of Rushing; as soon as you entered the hall you were expected to stick a fork in your patty, a spoon in your porridge plate and so on, otherwise anyone else could 'rush' them as well as his own. There was also Condescending, the word 'condescend' being perhaps a corruption of 'Can't you send'. No one in the junior house could condescend till he was in his third term, then he could pass the word down the table 'Condescend the sugar—or the milk—third-termer', and the milk or sugar had to be sent to him unless a fourth-termer or fifth-termer liked to intervene and condescend it for himself on the way. Thus a new boy was always like Tantalus, about to help himself from a bowl or jug which just as he was reaching for it would be harshly condescended away.

Sorley was more fortunate than MacNeice in arriving with two friends from prep. school—Arthur Bethune-Baker and Hugh Buss. Buss had won a Foundation Scholarship, reserved for the sons of clergy, and had been outstanding at King's College Choir School both at lessons and sports. He had won his scholarship a year earlier than Sorley, but had stayed on an extra year as head of the school and Senior Chorister, winning almost every honour there was to win. Sorley probably felt somewhat overawed by him. At any rate, he had very little contact with Buss once they reached Marlborough. However he did continue to be close friends with Bethune-Baker, a much quieter boy than Buss, who was not academically as brilliant though he excelled him in certain sports.

Comforting as it was to have a ready made friend, there was still a great deal to intimidate and bewilder Sorley in the elaborate school system. Marlborough differed from many public schools in having both Junior and Senior Houses, about 80 out of the 650 boys being in Junior Houses as 'a device for easing the transition from childhood to boyhood', but some Old Marlburians remember their time there as more painful than later on. Junior Houses were divided into 'In-College' Houses—A_1 and A_2—and 'Out-College'—Priory, Barton Hill, Upcot and Hermitage (boys from the latter being called S.O.Bs, or Small Out-House Boarders). Sorley entered A_1 House and remained 'In-College' throughout his career, for he later moved up to one of the six In-College Senior Houses, C_1 (the other five being C_2, C_3, B_1, B_2, B_3). There were also four Senior Out-Houses, Cotton, Littlefield, Preshute and Summerfield. It was generally thought more convenient to be In-College but more comfortable to be Out, since In-College Houses were mainly converted from older buildings not designed for school use. Marlborough had originally been intended for the sons of relatively poor men, who could not look forward to an affluent life and it had not basically changed by Sorley's time. Though there had been a gradual improvement of the hard conditions, the food was still poor, the dormitories, classrooms and day-rooms still crowded and the bathrooms still primitive. L.E. Upcott, an assistant master from 1875 to 1915, recalls:

> That time was an era of cold water. To shirk your cold tub in the morning, though the thermometer might be at freezing-point, was to jeopardize your social status. But of course small boys only stood at their basins and washed to the waist, though they might have been fagged by the bigger boys to fetch hot water. There was a bathroom to each house, and in my own house (C_1) the hot-bath list was made out by the captain of classroom and submitted to me: I remember being horrified by its inadequacy: I had myself been better supplied as a little boy at Sherbourne School.

Arriving from a comfortable middle-class home, with no experience of boarding-school, Sorley must have found these spartan conditions something of a shock. Yet he never complained, though he occasionally joked about them. His day began very early at 6.30 a.m. with a cold wash. Then there was early school from 7.05 a.m. until 7.50, followed by compulsory chapel. Sorley was already beginning to question conventional religion and his attitude towards it became increasingly ambivalent, as we shall see, but his views on chapel itself were fairly straightforward: 'I fear we are not so like Sidney and Beatrice [Webb] after all,' he wrote to a schoolfriend. 'For never once did I think of whiling away *the slow hours spent in Chapel* in the interests of religion, by pretending it was Parliament'. More soberly he asked, in a poem addressed to the same friend:

> And is the Chapel still a house of sin
> Where smiling men let false Religion in?

He was more light-hearted about breakfast, which followed chapel at 8.15 in that 'great bleak hall' as MacNiece
calls it: '[The soldiers] are fed twice as well as we are at
Marlborough,' Sorley told his parents after a visit to
Devizes barracks, 'bacon every morning for breakfast and
eggs for tea and as much butter and jam as they like'.
Breakfast for Marlburians usually consisted of porridge
(without sugar!) and a boiled egg or kipper, with bread
and tea. There was a College Steward, Mr Vile, and a
Butler, Mr Salter, beside numerous other servants who
waited on the boys. The bread was handed round in a
basket by a stout woman called Emma and was accompanied by a single pat of butter (known as 'spat' because
of the noise it made when flicked up at the ceiling!) The
boys generally supplemented it with their own jam or
'Lyall's syrup coloured gold', as Sorley wrote. They
would fill their so-called 'play-box' with as much food
as possible at the beginning of term and, when it ran
out, would resort to one of the two tuck-shops, between
which there was great rivalry and, according to Sorley,
some difference. Describing prefects in a satire on Marlborough, he writes:

On Sundays are there thirty chosen ones
    Who wear white ties, because their lives are white,
Who spurn the Wrong, nor eat Duck's damp cream buns,
    But eat fair Knapton's cakes and choose the Right?

Even new boys were allowed to visit the tuck-shops
before lunch, though only the Sixth were privileged to
do so after it. There may have been time for Sorley to
rush off to Duck or Knapton between breakfast and the
first prep. of the day, which began at 9.15 and lasted
half-an-hour. He was more likely to have succeeded after
morning school, which ended at noon on Fag Days. On
these whole schooldays there were also two periods
between 5 p.m. and 6.30. On half-holidays—Tuesdays,
Thursdays and Saturdays—there were no afternoon

lessons, but a fourth morning period at 12.20 ending just before lunch at 1.30.

Lunch itself was a more formal affair than breakfast. The boys had to stand and wait for grace to be said before they sat down at one of their two housetables. The housemaster, sitting at the head of one, and the second master at the head of the other would carve the meat, which was provided only once a day. The second course was usually something heavy like bread and butter pudding or 'Bolly' (roly-poly). The afternoon was devoted to games, cricket in the summer and rugger or hockey in the winter. On the whole Sorley disapproved of games at Marlborough because he felt that they so easily degenerated into 'a means of giving free play to the lower instincts of man'. He was not, and did not wish to become, competitive. Yet he enjoyed both playing and watching games, almost against his will. 'In spite of my intense desire to hate it, I always liked cricket,' he confessed. 'It was only school matches and watching them that ate my heart out and made me think of Francis Thompson's lines of ghastly genius:[1]

It is little I repair to the matches of the Southron folk,
Though my own red roses there may blow;
It is little I repair to the matches of the Southron folk,
Though the red roses crest the caps, I know.
For the field is full of shades as I near the shadowy coast,
And a ghostly batsman plays to the bowling of a ghost,
And I look through my tears on a soundless-clapping host
  As the run-stealers flicker to and fro, to and fro:
  O my Hornby and my Barlow long ago!

Francis T. was only a watcher of cricket and a player on Third like me. I remember when in A House I used to love watching school matches and keep the averages of now-forgotten Shaws. *So ist er in der welt.*[2] (*CL*)

[1] From Francis Thompson's poem 'At Lord's'.
[2] Literally, 'So it is in the world'.

Sorley was better at rugger, in which he played centre forward. He loved the 'sensation of complete physical subjugation and mental content' he derived from it. He also enjoyed hockey, particularly when it was played for pleasure rather than winning.

More than any of these team sports, however, Sorley loved running. He must have been one of the few boys to welcome the rain, which meant that games would be replaced by 'sweats', or cross-country runs. Most boys felt as J.P.T. Bury did, who has described a typical sweat in his article, 'A Day at Marlborough':

2.40 p.m. A long line of white and coloured jerseys stream down the road over Duck's Bridge (a popular misnomer) past the high-level station and up the Forest Hill, while the rain pours down incessantly. But the wind and rain are at their worst on the downs, and to the downs the house captain is particularly fond of sending his victims. It is 3 o'clock, and all the favourite tracks are covered: red, white, and blue, Preshute is going to Old Eagle; black and blue and blue and white, B_1 and B_3 to Rockley Warren or Rockley Copse; magenta and white, C_3's objective is Trainer's; red and blue, A House is content with First Post.

Sorley loved these 'sweats' through the rain, which to begin with in A House were relatively short. Years later in France a certain road 'hedged on one side only, with open ploughland to the right' reminded him of A House 'sweats' and his enthusiasm broke out anew:

It runs a little down hill till the road branches. Then half left up over open country goes our track, with the ground shelving away to right of us. Can you see it? The Toll House to the First Post on Trainers Down (old finishing point of A House sweats) on a small scale. There is something in the way that at the end of the hedge the road leaps up to the left into the beyond that puts me in mind of Trainers Down (as C House called it). It is what that turn into unhedged country and that leap promises, not what it achieves, that makes the likeness. It is nothing when you get up, no wildness, no openness. But there it remains to cheer me on each relief.

To the Master he wrote, 'O for a pair of shorts and my long loose coloured jersey—gules and argent—once again.'* The downs were to be Sorley's main source of inspiration for his poetry at Marlborough and running through the rain made them seem even more exhilerating, as the rhythm and imagery of the following poems shows:

> We swing ungirded hips,
> And lightened are our eyes,
> The rain is on our lips,
> We do not run for prize.
> We know not whom we trust
> Nor whitherward we fare
> But we run because we must
>   Through the great wide air.
>
> The waters of the seas
> Are troubled as by storm.
> The tempest strips the trees
> And does not leave them warm.
> Does the tearing tempest pause?
> Do the tree-tops ask it why?
> So we run without a cause
>   'Neath the big bare sky.
>
> The rain is on our lips,
> We do not run for prize.
> But the storm the water whips
> And the wave howls to the skies.

*Red and silver were Sorley's house colours.

The winds arise and strike it
And scatter it like sand,
And we run because we like it
Through the broad bright land.

Though obviously inspired by 'sweats', this poem was
written after Sorley left Marlborough, out of nostalgia
no doubt. There is a more direct reference to sweating
in a less serious poem written while still at school. Opening this piece with a description of a funeral, he continues:

And some strange sweaty creatures stop to see
On those bald heights—strange bare-kneed passers by,
With scarves about their necks that they may be
(Do they still think it?) Comely to the eye,
And say, In Marlborough they daily die,
And gape and pass on downwards to brew tea.

Tea was a great event in the lives of most Marlburians,
since they usually made it themselves from all kinds of
indigestible combinations such as sardines and sausages—
John Betjeman's favourite! 'Brewing', as it was called,
has been celebrated by more than one Marlburian,
usually with more zest than elegance:

I don't mind work—a little—
And I do love games a few;
But the chiefest joy of a Marlborough boy
Is a jolly stodgy Brew. (*Marlburian*, 1876)

Bury gives a more detailed, but no less enthusiastic
picture of the ritual:

4.30 p.m. Everywhere a clatter of knives and of plates,
a sizzling of sausages and a bubbling of kettles! From
the small boy in A House who possesses one bent
fork and a tin of apricots to the owner of a study
with a whole tea-service of his own, everyone feels
the need for food. Never do the rival firms of Duck
and [Knapton] do such a roaring trade as now between

47

the hours of 4 and 6. The little shops are thronged with those who are too lazy to cook sausages and make omelettes, and for whom a 3d meringue or a 2d chocolate walnut are equally attractive.

For those who had nothing left in their 'brew'-boxes and no money for Duck's or Knapton's delicacies, the college provided tea, though there were few wanting to eat dry bread or hard college biscuits (known as 'Kil Hallers'). Sorley, who believed that 'the stomach is the best procurer of enjoyment', is not likely to have attended this meal. Unfortunately he had to attend the next and similar meal at 6.45, which was compulsory for everyone but sixthformers. But he was probably too full of sausages and cakes to want college bread and 'spat'. Most of the boys sat looking at empty plates and rushed off as soon as the bell released them. There followed half-an-hour of freedom before evening prep., 'most feverish', according to Bury, in A House, where Sorley doubtless joined in with the general hubbub and threw paper darts with the rest. At 7.15, however, he had to settle down in A House Classroom for an hour's prep. under the supervision of a master. And if after that he was hungry, which he usually was, he could fill up on cocoa and 'Kil Hallers' at 8.15 p.m. House prayers followed at 8.30 and then for A House, who were not subjected to a second hour's prep., there was bed. There were six dormitories in A House and these were, according to Beverley Nichols, 'amusing places':

The general impression was rather cheerless—bare boards, big windows which always seemed to be open to the snow as well as to the sun, a long washing stand containing a blue basin for each boy, and ranged down the walls iron bedsteads, each covered with a scarlet counterpane, known as 'College Redder,' which was all the colour which the room possessed. Every night, at about quarter to nine, they started to fill

with shrieking boys, who continued shrieking till
9.15, when a bell rang and they knelt down (rather
out of breath) to pray. After their souls, and incident-
ally their lungs, were thus relieved, renewed excitement
was the order of the night until at 9.30 'lights out' was
sounded. The captains of dormitory then lined up,
looking very pink and clean, in their pyjamas, to say
good-night to the housemaster, and all the house was
silent.

In Sorley's dormitory, however, all was *not* silent, for
he was in popular demand as a story-teller and kept the
boys enthralled long after 'Lights Out' with the thrilling
adventures of a character called Jonathan Armstrong.
He had evidently retained his early love of story-telling.

Sorley could listen as well as entertain, however, and
on the whole he made a good, if at times difficult pupil.
Sir James Penny, who left only nine years before Sorley
arrived, said that form-work at Marlborough 'was quite
good fun—there was nearly always something to laugh
at'. And there is little doubt that Sorley found it so. As
a scholar he had come into the school about halfway up
in Shell B. His form-master, F.A.H. Atkey, was also new
to Marlborough in 1908. In spite of Atkey's impressive
academic record as a scholar of Pembroke College, he
was teased by the boys, to begin with at least. Sorley
called his English Literature classes 'Crow's Circus' or
'Pop's Panto' and often misbehaved with him. One of
his housemates remembers a conversation with their
housemaster, who found Sorley difficult to handle:

> 'Sorley, I'm sorry to hear that you have been rude to
>   Mr Atkey again.'
> 'Oh no, sir, not rude.'
> 'Well, Sorley, do you treat him with all due respect?'
> 'Oh yes, sir, all *due* respect.'
> 'What do you mean, Sorley, by all *due* respect? Do you
>   respect him for instance as you would the Master?'

'Oh no, sir, I place him on quite a different level, don't you?'

Though Atkey had read Classics at Oxford he had to teach English Literature at Marlborough as well. This was quite usual in Sorley's time, for English had only recently been included in the curriculum and there were not yet any specialists in the subject. It is noticeable that the youngest and newest Classics masters were generally expected to take it. French and German were on a similar footing and it is hardly surprising that when Sorley later visited Germany and France he had to start learning both languages anew. These two modern languages largely replaced Latin and Greek in the 'Modern' School, as it was called, the other subjects being Natural Sciences, Maths, History (chiefly modern), Geography and English Literature. English Composition was also compulsory, the assumption being that, if a boy was not a classicist, he could not write his own language properly. Music, Drawing, Bookkeeping, Shorthand and Science (known as 'stinks') were all extras and could be taken if wished. The Modern School tended to be looked down on by the 'Upper' School, which concentrated on classics to the exclusion of sciences. Sorley went through his whole 'Classical' career in 'Upper' School without being exposed to them. Beside Latin and Greek his other subjects were French, German, Maths, History (mainly ancient), Geography, Divinity, English Literature and Music. Predictably Sorley enjoyed his English classes, particularly when they progressed from Macaulay to Shakespeare's *Hamlet* and *The Tempest* in his third and fourth terms. In spite of his behaviour in Atkey's classes, he got a distinction for his work in English during his first term. Divinity, with its concentration on the Old Testament also interested him. Maths, however, he did not enjoy and his results throughout the school show that he never really mastered the subject. Latin he disliked, though he always found it easy, whereas he eventually learnt to love Greek—after he had stopped having to construe it for a 'pained Master'. His German teacher, Mr Lupton, found him 'a bit of a handful' and, as we have seen, Sorley did not learn a great deal in this class, though he had taken it voluntarily. 'It was certainly a tough struggle to induce Charles to work at anything that did not seem to him to come straight from the soul', said one of his teachers. From being near the top of the form in his last terms at King's College Choir School Sorley now slipped down during his four terms in Junior House to tenth, twelfth, fourteenth and sixteenth, respectively, in a class of between 24 and 27 boys. Buss was never lower than third in form, while his other prep.-schoolmate Bethune-Baker dropped right down to the bottom of the form in their second term, in Remove, and failed to go up with Buss and Sorley into Lower Fifth 1 in their third term. Nor did he go up with them into Lower Fifth 1 in their fourth and final term in Junior House.

Sorley had C.A. Emery for form-master as well as housemaster in his second term. His other form-masters during his first two years were A.R. Gidney, whom he got to know much better later on, and M.H. Gould. Gould was an eccentric, whom the boys loved. They would boo him loudly, whenever he entered the form-room, and even when he entered their studies. 'He was a funny old bird,' one of his students remembered. Sorley had Gould for two terms and recalled his time with him affectionately. 'Personally I found that the best time at M.C. was the earliest,' he wrote to a friend, 'the days under Gould'.

Certainly to begin with the school 'absorbed him completely' in his mother's words:

He had a period of hero-worship, very little qualified by criticism, for its demigods among the boys and masters; he abounded in the mysteries of its etiquette

51

and slang; and he would pore by the hour over the blue School List, declaring he knew by headmark most of the boys in it—which may very well have been the case, as he had a quick memory for names and faces. His enthusiasms were always breaking forth in brilliant generalizations, which were as often cheerfully and relentlessly shelved. So at this time he was certain that there was nothing to beat the public school system: it was the finest in the world.

The 'demigods among the boys' in Sorley's time were still mainly the athletes, though the Master, Frank Fletcher, had tried very hard to change this. It was undoubtedly Cotton who had elevated games to their central position at Marlborough, with his emphasis on their 'manly and healthy' nature in his letter to parents of 1853. J.A. Mangan argues in a very thorough study of the subject, that Athleticism goes with Imperialism and quotes the following lines from 'Carmen Marlburiense', a college song, to prove his point:

> Be strong, Elevens, to bowl and shoot,
> Be strong, O Regiment of the foot,
> With ball of skin or leather,
> Stand for the Commonwealth together.

During the second half of the nineteenth century, while imperialism was at its height, there is little doubt that athletes were considered superior to scholars. Sir Douglas Savory, who arrived at Marlborough in 1891, confirms that 'the real power was exercised by the athletes—boys who, because they got into the Eleven or the Fifteen were made captain of their houses. It is surprising how much athletics were exalted and schoolwork despised'. (D. Savory, *Sixty Years Ago*, p. 215). When Frank Fletcher arrived in 1903 he was appalled by the glorification of athletics, and tried to establish the powers of the prefects over the athletes. Sir James Penny, who had been at Marlborough four years when Fletcher arrived, saw the gradual diminishing of the athletes' dominance, but he felt that athletes were still worshipped and that it was natural that they should be—'athletic prowess, which anyone can see, . . . impress[es] boys more than book work'. Fletcher doubtless realised this after a time for he hoped that Penny, when Senior Prefect, would help win the boys' respect by getting into the First Fifteen! Pat Amps, who arrived in 1906, says that in his time the Senior Prefect was considered less important than the Captain of Cricket or Rugger. The athletes became 'bloods', he recalls, much sooner than the scholars, some of whom never became 'bloods'. George Turner, who was Senior Prefect during Amps' and Sorley's time never achieved this honour and probably never wished to. Sorley, who became sufficiently good at both games and work to escape the problem, had no doubt of the dominance of athletes: 'At Marlborough,' he wrote to Atkey, 'we were always encouraged to despise and reject such as knew the first line of the *Odyssey* and the *C[armen] S[aeculare]*, and to love, honour, and obey such as were better than us at hockey'. On another occasion, however, he seems to admit that the situation was not quite so clear-cut and that scholastic prowess was also likely to impress the younger boys: 'One can rise to a big position' at Marlborough, he argues, 'and have all one's words taken as gold, without knowing anything more of the world than in one case dead phrases from a dead language, in another how to hold a bat straight'.

He had himself, as a small boy in A House, watched the First Eleven cricketers with awe and no doubt he had worshipped them. He seems in all things to have been a healthy, normal schoolboy and hero-worship was a natural first stage in his career at Marlborough. His friends found him a pleasant, outgoing companion and did not discern that he had a secret life in the imagination. But it is fairly certain from the competence of his verse technique two years later that he was continuing to write poetry. His mother said that 'as he grew older he became more and more reserved about his writing'. No examples of his work have survived from these first four terms, but then as a Junior he could hardly hope to be published in the school magazine and there were no other outlets.

As Mrs Sorley wrote, school life absorbed him completely at first and if he was homesick he did not show it, though he was very happy to get home at the end of his first term for four weeks' Christmas holiday. Then there were three more weeks at Easter and in Summer 1909 his parents paid their first visit to Marlborough. Sorley insisted that they came, not for Speech Day, which was the usual practice, but earlier in the term when the countryside was fresh and green. Seven weeks of summer holidays followed, during which Sorley had the excitement of a first visit to France. The family, who were all keen cyclists, took their bicycles with them and rode along the coast of Normandy, ending up at a small hotel at Veules-Les-Roses. Sorley, who was as outspoken as his mother, said it was the rottenest country he had ever seen, but the finest holiday he had ever had. Returning to Marlborough in September 1909, he was no longer a new 'bug' but one of the oldest boys in A House. It was his last term there, for in January 1910 he entered a Senior House.

4
Marlborough, 1910-1911

When Sorley entered a Senior House in January 1910, he found himself with more freedom both in work and games. In A House he had been protected and supervised almost the whole time, but he was now expected to show more initiative and to prove that he could use his liberty responsibly. The Senior Houses were, in general, far more autonomous, being virtually run by the prefects, or 'captains' as they were called at Marlborough. The housemaster's role was now that of a supervisor, rather than a nurse. Sorley greatly appreciated this comparative freedom, though he did not always use it sensibly. For the first time in his life he was expected to make decisions for himself and the sensation was a heady one. From being overawed by the school and its senior members, he now became something of a critic and a rebel, as we shall see.

Sorley was delighted to find that his Senior House was one of the oldest at Marlborough—C_1. He appreciated it's beautiful setting in the ancient seat of the Seymours and its proximity to the Adderley Library, where he began to spend hours reading. As Beverley Nichols recalls, it was 'a most lovable place. There was an air of attractive mustiness about it' which he grew to need as essential to his wellbeing. 'There were six tall windows looking out on to the lawns and terraces outside [C] House, with its capacious, cut bushes, its sundial, and its tall trees that seemed never to cease to wave in the wind, and were noisy with the chattering of the rooks when the sun was going down'. Sorley was particularly proud of C_1's 'long intellectual and literary traditions both in housemasters and members' which he hoped to follow. C_1 was certainly a desirable house to get into and Sorley was probably right in claiming that it was 'the most typically Marlburian of all houses at Marlborough, though I says it as shouldn't'. No one, he believed, 'was really worth serious attention unless he was in C_1. It is a prejudice I have never been able to give us;... but I entered the house while it was still *Teucro duce et auspice Teucro* (Teucer being G.C. Turner), and that explains it'. George Turner was Senior Prefect of Marlborough as well as Head of C_1 in 1910 and undoubtedly one of Sorley's 'demigods'. Both a Foundation Scholar and Senior Scholar, he was a good classicist and left for Magdalen College, Oxford, at the end of Sorley's second term in C_1, returning later as an assistant master, then as Master (1926-39). 'I think I have never told you how much I admired Charles when we were boys together', Turner wrote to Mrs Sorley years afterwards. As he goes on to say, however, 'it was a distant admiration and unexpressed since I respected though I never in my heart endorsed school convention; I was a senior boy, rather absurdly important in my own and in some others' eyes, and Charles was a newcomer to the House'.

Sorley may have been new to C_1, but he quickly made friends there. Col. N.J. Awdry, a contemporary from B House, says that houses were very insular in those days and that one's friends tended to come from one's own house. Added to this there was Sorley's prejudice that no one was really worth serious attention unless he was in C_1. Fortunately Arthur Bethune-Baker, Sorley's Choir School friend, moved up with him into C_1 and also caught up with him in Lower Fifth 1. Bethune-Baker, the only child of a Cambridge don, seems to have been an unusual boy. Sorley found him 'very jolly' to be with and admired him for his 'invariably cheerful self-denial'. Though not as successful at football as he had been at prep. school, 'he always seemed just as pleased with the success of those who had outplaced him'. Sorley never remembered him trying to run down his weaker contemporaries, as so many of the boys did to glorify themselves. Yet he was not a prig, 'because it was all so natural with him'.

With Sorley and Bethune-Baker in both C_1 and Lower Fifth 1 was Herbert Leslie Ridley, who became Sorley's closest friend at Marlborough. Eight months older than Sorley, Ridley had entered Marlborough the term before him in Summer 1908. Though not a Scholar, Ridley was clever and in his second term came top of the class, winning the form prize. (Sorley had come tenth in class that same term.) Ridley was also something of an athlete, becoming Captain of the First Eleven Hockey in 1912. When Sorley began to share a study with him he revealed a more boisterous side to his nature, which caused Sorley to seek refuge elsewhere. 'I know those publishers' catalogues well,' he wrote to another friend who was wondering what book to choose for a prize, 'and used to spend hours in their company when R[idley] had banished me from my study by singing "The Girl in the Taxi"'! Yet when Sorley remembered him afterwards he forgot the irritations and grew quite nostalgic:

> Ridley with whom I brewed, 'worked', and shared a study, and quarrelled absolutely unceasingly for over three years. We have so thoroughly told each other all each other's faults and oddities for so long a time that nothing now could part·our friendship. (*CL*)

To Sorley, the Scot, Ridley was 'the best type of Englishman: whose gold lies hid and is never marketed'. He reminded Sorley of one of the noble, modest heroes in Hardy's earlier novels, Giles Winterbourne in particular. True to this image Ridley won an M.C. in the First World War and was killed in action near Ypres in 1917.

Sorley did not share a study with Ridley immediately on entering C_1, since studies were in short supply. When a boy first entered a Senior House he normally spent most of his day in 'Upper School'. Frank Fletcher was proud of this 'peculiarly Marlburian institution', but

MacNeice, who experienced Upper School, was less enthusiastic:

> It had been built about 1850 and, though enormously
> large, hardly seemed like a building at all. It was just a
> great tract of empty air, cold as the air outside but
> smelling of stables, enclosed by four thin walls and a
> distant roof. One half of the floor was covered with
> desks and benches, the other half was empty; there
> were only two doors and two fires. These were coal
> fires and radiated heat for not more than two or three
> yards. One fire was called Big Fire and reserved for
> less than twenty boys who were the oligarchy; the other
> fire, Little Fire, was open to the rest of us who num-
> bered about a hundred. To be elected to Big Fire was
> a great honour but could only be hoped for by
> athletes or by boys so stupid that they had remained
> in Upper School longer than the normal span; if you
> had any brains you were soon moved on elsewhere.

MacNeice goes on to describe the somewhat barbaric
rites of Upper School, such as mass canings, 'scavenging',
and 'basketing'. Sorley, however, did not have to face
these. As a scholar he was privileged to go straight into
the Bradleian, a quieter and more studious place than
Upper School. George Turner, who had also been in the
Bradleian, thought it 'a cosy but doubtfully wise seg-
regation'. Sorley must have enjoyed the greater degree
of independence given to boys there, and their eccentric
guardian, whom Turner describes:

> There we were looked after by the Master who lived
> above Bradleian Arches, the brilliant and lovable John
> O'Regan (known as Pat); product of Ireland and
> Balliol, a rich mixture. He gave splendid teas in his
> room, where he kept a chameleon fed on flies and a
> mongoose fed on eggs. (G.C. Turner, 'Scattered Mem-
> ories', *The Marlburian*, Lent Term, 1966, p. 22)

Frank Fletcher found Pat O'Regan 'essentially out of the ordinary' and the boys, particularly the intelligent ones, were stimulated by this. O'Regan, who had founded the History School at Marlborough, taught his subject with an enthusiasm and grasp that made it vivid to his pupils. There is little doubt that Sorley would have responded well to O'Regan, whom he later visited at the curious house he had built for himself in the style of a Roman villa. Another side of O'Regan's character that would have appealed to Sorley was his interest in poetry, which he encouraged the boys to write. Siegfried Sassoon, who came to Marlborough in 1902 and stayed only two years, remembered O'Regan as one of his sole consolations there:

> Sometimes he read us a little poetry, and when we had an odd twenty minutes to fill in he would, if the spirit moved him, tell us to write some ourselves, and offer a prize of half a crown. Thank you, Mr O'Regan, for those half-crowns (I nearly always won them). You were the only person at Marlborough who ever asked me to write poetry. The first time I won the prize you had my verses framed and hung them in the form-room, so for the sake of old times I will reproduce them here:

> > My life at school is fraught with care,
> > Replete with many a sorrow.
> > When evening shadows fall I dare
> > Not think about to-morrow.

> > The extra lesson doth correct
> > My wandering attention;
> > And other things which I expect
> > It might give pain to mention.

> > But extra lessons cannot kill,
> > And blows are not so hard

That they will end the life of this
Ambitious little bard.

After leaving O'Regan's tutelage in the Bradleian
Sorley probably spent a brief period in his House Classroom, which was the next step up to a study. There,
with about twenty other boys from C_1 he would do his
prep. under the supervision of his housemaster. Once he
got his study, which as we know he shared with Ridley,
he would move out of C_1 building to one of the study
blocks, for there were only two or three studies within
each House and these were reserved for House Captains
and Prefects.

Sorley was now in the middle of the school, no longer
a baby but not yet a 'blood'. He had left the protection
of A House and was, therefore, more exposed to the
usual demands of a public school. Fagging had never
been very rigorous at Marlborough and under Fletcher it
was even less so, but there was still a certain amount of
it for younger boys in senior houses. Sixth form boys
had a right to fag anyone, but they were held in check
by a book of rules setting out their rights and duties.
MacNeice tells harrowing stories about 'coal-fagging',
when he had to scrabble about in an unlit cellar trying to
find lumps of coal in the dust, and 'milk-fagging' when
he had to carry eight mugs of milk or more across the
courtyard and up the stairs without spilling a drop. But
those who were at Marlborough in Sorley's day found it
less arduous. They were generally set fairly easy tasks,
such as cleaning a prefect's football boots or cricket
gear, cooking a sausage for his tea, running to the tuck-
shop for him ('bull-fagging') or retrieving cricket balls in
the nets. In spite of such minor irritations Sorley found
life in the middle school most enjoyable. 'His attitude
towards the school, though essentially loyal and filial,
developed in breadth and humour', his mother records.
Though he began to improve academically, at the same

time he grew even more mischievous. When wishing a friend a 'good' last term, he added—'I *don't* mean well-behaved'. There is no doubt that he was becoming something of a rebel. When Dr Wynne Willson arrived in 1911 to take over the mastership from Frank Fletcher his first impression was that Sorley 'was a rebel against a new régime'. Sorley himself implies that his rebelliousness sprang from a deeper criticism of the public school system, which he was now beginning to question. He was already formulating the ideas which he expressed two years later in his poem 'What You Will':

> O come and see, it's such a sight,
> So many boys all doing right:
> To see them underneath the yoke,
> Blindfolded by the elder folk,
> Move at a most impressive rate
> Along the way that is called straight.
> O, it is comforting to know
> They're in the way they ought to go.
> But don't you think it's far more gay
> To see them slowly leave the way
> And limp and loose [*sic*] themselves and fall?
> O, that's the nicest thing of all.
> I love to see this sight, for then
> I know they are becoming men
> And they are tiring of the shrine
> Where things are really not divine.

The more Sorley questioned the school system, the fonder he grew of such solitary pursuits as running, cycling and walking. Apart from the compulsory Sunday walk, when boys had to attend 'distant call' at the 'Four Miler', or other landmarks, Sorley often roamed the countryside by himself with a favourite book in his hand. He has left a description of the 'best walk [he] ever had':

I went out along the downs almost to Swindon, [he wrote to his parents] but turned off into a village known as Liddington, and made a life-long friend of the publican, whose heart is in his back garden, so that I left Liddington laden with bouquets which it was no child's work carrying in the heat of the day. I then scaled Liddington Castle which is no more a castle than I am, but a big hill with a fine Roman camp on the top, and a view all down the Vale of the White Horse to the north, and the Kennet valley to the south. I sat down there for about an hour reading *Wild Life in a Southern County* with which I had come armed—the most appropriate place in the world to read it from, as it was on Liddington Castle that Richard Jefferies wrote it and many others of his books, and as it is Jefferies' description of how he saw the country from there. Jefferies, I suppose you know, was a Wiltshire man, and was brought up at Coate, now a suburb of Swindon, not ten miles north of Marlborough. Indeed there are to be found horrible critics with a passion for labelling everything, who refer to the country between Swindon and Marlborough as the Richard-Jefferies land. I then walked along a hog's back to Aldbourne where I had tea and returned in the evening across the Aldbourne downs. (*CL*)

For a time Richard Jefferies became the first in a line of 'favourite prophets' or 'deities' for Sorley. His yearning for Jefferies' vision and wisdom shows in his own aims in poetry at this time:

RICHARD JEFFERIES
(Liddington Castle)

I see the vision of the Vale
    Rise teeming to the rampart Down,
The fields and, far below, the pale
    Red-roofédness of Swindon town.

But though I see all things remote,
    I cannot see them with the eyes
With which ere now the man from Coate
    Looked down and wondered and was wise.

He knew the healing balm of night,
    The strong and sweeping joy of day,
The sensible and dear delight
    Of life, the pity of decay.

And many wondrous words he wrote,
    And something good to man he showed,
About the entering in of Coate,
    There, on the dusty Swindon road.

Sorley considered Jefferies 'the greatest of English vision-
aries', greater even than Blake, whom he grew to love
later on. He identified with Jefferies' love of the downs
and felt, like Jefferies, that he 'climbed great hills that
should overlook the sea, but [one] could see no sea.
Only the whole place is like a vast sea-shell where [one]
can hear the echoes of the sea that has once filled it . . .
One can really *live* up there!' He continued to love his
runs across the downs, in the rain, partly because they
helped him to escape the confines of school life and
partly because they gave rise to visions of his own:

When the rain is coming down,
And all Court is still and bare,
And the leaves fall wrinkled, brown,
Through the kindly winter air,
And in tattered flannels I
'Sweat' beneath a tearful sky,
And the sky is dim and grey,
And the rain is coming down,
And I wander far away
From the little red-capped town:
There is something in the rain
That would bid me to remain:

There is something in the wind
That would whisper, 'Leave behind
All this land of time and rules,
Land of bells and early schools.
Latin, Greek and College food
Do you precious little good.
Leave them: if you would be free
Follow, follow, after me!'

When I reach 'Four Miler's' height,
And I look abroad again
On the skies of dirty white
And the drifting view of rain,
And the bunch of scattered hedge
Dimly swaying on the edge,
And the endless stretch of downs
Clad in green and silver gowns;
There is something in their dress
Of bleak barren ugliness,
That would whisper, 'You have read
Of a land of light and glory:
But believe not what is said.
'Tis a kingdom bleak and hoary,
Where the winds and tempests call
And the rain sweeps over all . . .' ('Rain')

It may have been on one of Sorley's solitary walks or
sweats across the downs that he first met another 'interpreter' of their mysteries—John Bain, an assistant master.
For he was never taught by Bain, yet knew him well
enough to write a poem about him when Bain left the
school in 1913:

J. B.

There's still a horse on Granham hill,
And still the Kennet moves, and still
Four Miler sways and is not still.
But where is her interpreter?

The downs are blown into dismay,
The stunted trees seem all astray,
Looking for someone clad in grey
     And carrying a golf-club thing;

Who, them when he had lived among,
Gave them what they desired, a tongue.
Their words he gave them to be sung
Perhaps were few, but they were true.

The trees, the downs, on either hand,
Still stand, as he said they would stand.
But look, the rain in all the land
     Makes all things dim with tears of him.

And recently the Kennet croons,
And winds are playing widowed tunes.
—He has not left our 'toun o' touns,'
     But taken it away with him!

This is scarcely more than clever occasional verse, but
the sentiment was deeply felt. For Sorley greatly admired
John Bain, who had become known over the years at
school as the 'Marlborough Laureate', and thought him
'the greatest living poet in his way'. He was particularly
impressed by Bain's refusal to publish anything, though
as he told his parents, Bain wrote 'wonderful verse in
seven languages'.

Sorley may have met Bain through O'Regan, who was
a close friend, or at one of the breakfast parties Bain
frequently gave. But it is most likely that they met on
the downs during their long walks. There is no doubt
that once they had met Sorley would have found much
to admire and encourage. Not only did Bain openly
write poetry in an ethos that was not particularly sympathetic towards it, but he also wrote it mainly about
the downs. Sorley especially admired Bain's 'splendid
new song'—the *Scotch Marlburian* written for a school
prize-giving. Though Sorley himself never wrote in Scots

dialect he identified with Bain in this respect too and noted that he was 'a Scotchman *of course*'. The opening stanza of this song shows that Sorley introduced some of its phrases into certain of his poems, as well as indicating a common subject matter:

> O Marlb'rough she's a town o' towns,
> Ye maun say that an' mair
> Ye that hae trod on her green downs,
> An snuffed her Wiltshire air
> A weary road ye'll hae to tramp,
> Afore ye match the green
> O' Savernake an' Barbury Camp,
> An' a' that lies atween.

Sorley would also have been attracted to Bain by his mild eccentricity. He was, as his son put it, 'oddly informal for the period' and most approachable. Though well qualified to teach the Classical Sixth, he chose to teach the Army Class, who were generally considered 'duds', and his teaching methods were somewhat unconventional for the time. Bain was critical of the public school system, though he loved Marlborough, and was *not* obsessed by games, though good at them. In these respects too Sorley would have shared his independent attitude.

Bain, an essentially modest man, was delighted by Sorley's poem, which appeared in *The Marlburian*, but could not discover its authorship. It was not until Sorley composed a second poem (see page 00), this time a verse-letter to Bain from France, which he signed 'The Voice', that Bain discovered the poet's identity through the handwriting. He replied immediately:

> From far away there comes a Voice,
> Singing its song across the sea—
> A song to make man's heart rejoice—
> Of Marlborough and the Odyssey.

A Voice that sings of Now and Then,
  Of minstrel joys and tiny towns,
Of flowering thyme and fighting men
  Of Sparta's sands and Marlborough's Downs

God grant, dear Voice, one day again
  We see those Downs in April weather,
And sniff the breeze and smell the rain,
  And stand in C House Porch together.

Sorley's friendship with Bain alone shows that his increasing love of isolation did not make him a recluse. He still joined in enthusiastically with communal activities, continuing to play rugger and hockey and even becoming captain of the House cricket team, albeit the Third Eleven. More than games or sports, however, he enjoyed the Officers Training Corps, which he joined in the Michaelmas term of 1910. Until 1908 the school Corps had been known as the Volunteers, or 'Bugshooters'. With the introduction of the Territorials, they were renamed Officers Training Corps and recognised as potential Territorial or Special Reserve officers. As such they were trained for Certificate 'A', which consisted of a written exam in tactics and a practical exam in tactics, drill, map-reading and weapon training at Section Commander level. For every 'efficient' cadet the government made a grant, which enabled the Corps to build up its supply of arms and equipment. The new status of the Corps and the enthusiasm of the Master Frank Fletcher made recruiting easier and by the time Sorley entered it two years later almost every able-bodied boy in the school had joined. The Corps commander, Major A.H. Wall, was also Sorley's housemaster during his first term in C_1 and Sorley had his reservations about him. He was, for instance, very relieved to find, when setting off to take Certificate 'A' at Devizes that the Major was not going to accompany them, as he told his parents:

We started off at nine o'clock in uniform and O.T.C. greatcoats (most comfortable things), with Sergt-Major Barnes (wot we didn't tip) and not (thank Heaven!) the Major to look after us. I got a pew next Barnes and I was sure of an interesting drive.

The Sergeant-Major, who was popular with the boys, entertained Sorley and the other cadets in the bus with one of his famous stories about a labourer wrongfully hanged for the murder of a coach-driver. Barnes was a first-class soldier with seventeen years' service in the Wiltshire Regiment behind him, but, as one of his cadets recalled 'he had the heart of a boy and loved having his leg pulled—and retaliating'. One of his off-duty occupations was watching school rugger matches, when he would roar out in his tremendous voice, 'Now then, Marlborough, another try!' and the whole school would roar back. Barnes had another, more serious, side to his nature—a passion for correctness. He would write out all the adjutant's orders in a beautiful copperplate hand and ask one of the cadet officers to check the spelling. If there was one mistake he would rewrite the whole page.

Barnes amused Sorley greatly at Devizes barracks by his indignation at the pampering the soldiers received: 'When he was in the same barracks twenty years ago he had existed for weeks on "skilly", i.e. dry bread soaked with tea'. Sorley had just enjoyed a very good lunch when Barnes told him this and did not object at all to the soldiers' splendid food. In fact he had enjoyed himself so much that he wished 'they had not been so kind in marking me so that I might have tried again in the summer'. He quite envied the three failures!

Field Days he also enjoyed greatly, finding them 'much more the kind of thing' he liked than Sports Days. On these occasions the Corps would catch a very early train to a given spot, where several public schools would meet. They would then take sides and carry out a manoeuvre, such as attacking the Clifton Suspension Bridge. Sorley loved the chance to be out in the open all day and paid more attention to the landscape than to the military objective. Beverley Nichols, who enjoyed Field Days for similar reasons, has given a lively if exaggerated description of them:

> Of course, from a military point of view they were a farce; all one did was to lie on a hill, chewing grass and occasionally firing blank into a tuft of gorse, watching the little cloud of smoke it made and one or two yellow blossoms fluttering to the ground. Now and then the signal would be given to advance—against whom or why, no one knew; but one could always walk, and it relieved the monotony. And then there were the meals, which lasted an inordinate time; always the same pork pies and chocolate and a slice of plumcake, and anything else that one liked to provide. Finally, there was the march home, usually through the tall avenues of [Savernake] Forest with the band playing 'Colonel Bogey' and the boys trying to drown the bass with 'Glory, Glory, Alleluliah'.

Following the march back, which continued in full swing up the High Street, there was a Corps 'Brew', either in the town's Corn Exchange or in Upper School, which was often used for entertainments. Sorley enjoyed these 'Brews' greatly and usually took an active part in them. Mrs Lupton, the wife of his German master, remembered one such occasion well and wrote to tell his sister about it:

> Your brother, an elegant figure in uniform, was given the job of making a speech bringing in the names of all the guests of the Corps that day, with a few appropriate words about each.
> He was doing it admirably, giving rise to bursts of laughter, when he came to—'We are proud today in

having Colonel X among us—he is—' Then came a frantic whisper from Major Wall, centre back, 'Sorley— He isn't here—couldn't come!' Your brother was for a brief moment deflated . . . Then quickly recovering himself, 'I learn that Colonel X was not able after all to be present, but we have Mrs Lupton with us and that is just as good.

Sorley with his strong self-awareness thought the Corps Brews were 'the most perfect type of a Mutual Admiration Evening. We go away thinking each of us personally is the smartest member of the smartest corps in the world'. He was always suspcious of self-importance, in himself or anyone else, and was therefore delighted when some- thing happened to deflate the Corps, after one such evening:

But this time a very fortunate incident occurred on the way home. The band were so puffed up by the nice things that had been said about them, that they were making a great deal more noise than was right at 10 p.m. The result was that the first horse we met bolted. We were marching on the left of the road and the horse was on the right, and you know how broad the High Street is. There was no danger; even the horse was not very frightened. But the College Corps were! In a second we were all on the pavement, making for the wall; and we had been marching at attention under military discipline. I have never seen anything so disgraceful; but it just reminded us that we weren't all Wellingtons yet. I think this should be arranged to happen after every Corps Brew. The humorous horse, when he saw us beginning to venture back into line again, settled down into a trot; and we marched back to bed trying hard to pretend it was a dream.

Sorley feared taking himself too seriously and he was determined that the O.T.C. should not make him do so.

His attitude towards the Corps was, therefore, rather ironic, even towards the annual camp, which he looked forward to. 'I hear that a *very* select group of public schools will by this time be enjoying the Camp,' he wrote to the Master from the British army in France. 'May they not take it too seriously! Seein' as 'ow all training is washed out as soon as you turn that narrow street corner at Boulogne'. A photograph of Sorley sitting, a tin mug in his hand, a broad grin on his face and bare feet suggests that he enjoyed camp greatly and did not take it too seriously. He is unlikely to have enjoyed parades quite so much. There were two a week—a short one of three-quarters of an hour in civilian clothes after Hall and a long parade of one and a half hours in Corps uniform. There was one occasion when a parade became exciting, for in 1911 the Corps went to the Coronation Review and spent the day parading in Windsor Park. Sorley was probably as proud as the rest of them when King George V, noticing their conspicuous green berets, asked who they were and expressed his approval. On the whole, however, Sorley's attitude towards the O.T.C. was satirical, as the following lines suggest:

And is there still a Folly called the Corps
Allowed out twice a week and thinking then
It's learning how to kill its fellow-men?

Just over a month after Sorley first joined the Corps in September 1910, something much more serious happened, which affected him deeply. One Sunday early in November, Sorley, Bethune-Baker and another friend, De Sausmarez, were planning to take the 'distant call' walk together. Bethune-Baker had been feeling very unwell all day, but would not let Sorley or De Sausmarez spoil their afternoon by staying with him. On their return they found he had reported sick. A few days later, on 8 November 1910, he died of meningitis. At the time Sorley 'took it very quietly', his mother said, but it is clear from later evidence that his friend's death at such an impressionable age had a profound effect on him. In 1914 he wrote to Mrs Bethune-Baker to tell her what an increasing influence all his remembrances of Arthur, during the three years they knew each other well, had had on him. This was Sorley's first direct contact with death and it may explain his preoccupation with the subject, though as usual he turns this into a joke:

> If the Lord God were to come down from heaven and offer me any gift I liked in reward for the service I had done to him, I should choose to be a Widow. It must be simply grand. Haven't you often prayed—I have—that people you like may die, in order that you may have the luxury of mourning and being wept with and pitied? The dead are after all the supreme aristocrats. And widowhood or any other state involving a close connection with or dependence on Death gives one a magnificent standing. The lady you mention reminds me always of that child in Laurence Housman's* poem which ends:

> > But in another week they said
> > That friendly pinkfaced man was dead.
> > 'How sad . . .,' they said, 'the best of men . . .'
> > So I said too, 'How Sad'; but then
> > Deep in my heart I thought with pride
> > 'I know a person who has died.'

The term Bethune-Baker died Sorley came sixteenth in form again—another indication that he was more affected by his friend's death than he showed. For in the two previous terms, Lent and Summer 1910, he had risen to third and eighth respectively and was making much better progress. And in the two terms following the death he rose again to sixth in class on both occasions, also winning the Congreve Prize for General Culture. By

*The poem is actually by Frances Cornford.

Michaelmas 1910 he had reached the Upper Fifth and his form-master was again Atkey, with whom he remained for his last three terms in the middle school. Atkey had by this time greatly improved as a disciplinarian and Sorley now enjoyed being in his form. He grew to respect Atkey and probably identified with him, for he considered Atkey 'too much of a freelance in thoughtful matters to come to his own' at Marlborough. Sorley, as we have seen, was becoming increasingly independent in his own beliefs. As he got to know Atkey better he found him 'a wonderfully nice man . . . the sanest humanest man in Common Room' and kept in touch with him long after they had both left Marlborough. Atkey died on the Somme in 1916.

Sorley counted Atkey among the three best assistant masters at Marlborough. Geoffrey Bickersteth was one of the other two. Bickersteth had come to the College in 1909 from Charterhouse and Christ Church, Oxford. Though his main interest was Italian literature, he was also very keen on English literature and when George Turner persuaded A.R. Gidney to start a Senior Literary Society in 1910 for the Upper Sixth, Bickersteth was among the first members. As a junior master, however, he regretted that the younger boys had not similar opportunities to discuss English Literature. So that when Gidney told him that one of his pupils, Sorley, showed great talent in his verse translations from Latin and Greek,* Bickersteth seized the excuse and formed the Junior Literary Society in October 1911, mainly for Sorley's benefit.

Sorley had not been taught by Bickersteth, but he quickly grew to admire his wide knowledge and his stimulating talk, as his notes to the Junior Literary Society show. Describing a paper given by the secretary, E.W. Marshall, on Milton, Sorley concludes:

*See *Collected Poems* for an example of one of these translations.

for the excellent discussion which followed Mr Bicker-steth suggested that he had over-praised Lycidas:—as an elegy, he said, it was marred by that anti-Catholic outburst, and pedantic classical allusions, smacking of the notebook and lecture-room. After a short discussion on the merits of the other great elegies, he finished the meeting appropriately by the stirring lines at the conclusion of Shelley's Adonais, which the Society agreed was the best of them all.

Sorley responded readily to anyone who questioned received truths, as Bickersteth did. In his turn Bickersteth appreciated Sorley's 'personality, so rich, so extraordin-arily lovable and so intensely alive'.* He felt that in the 'Song of the Ungirt Runner' Sorley had 'a picture of himself in shorts on the Marlborough Downs. And that closing rhythm, of which Meredith was so fond, recalls to me many and many an argument I've had with him over Meredith and Masefield'. To begin with Bickersteth had had to convert Sorley from Browning to Meredith (Masefield came later). Sorley's first paper to the Junior Literary Society had been on Browning, a favourite with many budding poets who welcome his swinging rhythms and colloquial language. Bickersteth made Sorley realise that there was a 'lack of *earth*' in Browning, whereas Meredith's poetry was closer to nature: 'I have often tried to save people,' Sorley wrote later, 'from the dusty intellectualism of *Rabbi Ben Ezra* and try and turn them on to the windy elemental strength of *Hard Weather* or other of Meredith's poems'. He came to believe with Bickersteth that with Meredith poetry 'returned to the earth', which Tennyson had vulgarised with the artificial-ity of his 'paltry and superficial' work. There is no doubt that Meredith influenced Sorley, whose earliest poem 'The Tempest' had already revealed his interest in 'windy

*Bickersteth also appreciated Sorley's sister, Jean, whom he met and married after Charles's death.

elemental strength'. He realised that some of his adol-
escent poems had 'too much copy from Meredith' in
them, especially these lines of 'Autumn Dawn':

> Earth is at length bedrid. She is
> Supinest of the things that be:
> And stilly, heavy with long years,
> Brings forth such days in dumb regret,
> Immortal days, that rise in tears,
> And cannot, though they strive to, set.

These are skilful and striking lines, but they lack the
simplicity of Sorley's later, more original verse.

Another paper delivered by Sorley, comparing Burns
and Scott suggests that he still retained a sense of his
Scottish origins. Having volunteered to give yet another
paper, on Blake, he became 'very keen on him indeed',
not so much on the 'slightly ingleneuk earlier works' as
the 'much more powerful later ravings'. But perhaps there
was not enough 'earth' in Blake either, for he never
became one of Sorley's 'deities'.

Yet there was something rather akin to Blake in
Sorley, which Bickersteth immediately recognised—a combination of mysticism and canny, good sense. Reading
Ethel Sidgwick's *Promise* years later, Bickersteth was
reminded of Sorley by the following description of
Antoine, who has just shown his grandfather M. Lemaure
a manuscript of his own musical composition:

> M. Lemaure bowed his head, unable to do more. The
> audacity almost appalled him, to fling oneself at
> thirteen on these unknown seas of pain. He knew,
> looking backward, that his own powers had sprang
> evenly and easily; he had known physical hardship in
> his youth—but no spiritual tempests until years later
> than this; yet this little boy, placed in ease and tranquil-

ity such as he had never known, had already anticipated the sorrows of life to this point.

Sorley continued to write poems, encouraged and stimulated by Geoffrey Bickersteth's interest in him. It was not until he left the Junior Literary Society for the Senior, however, that any of his poems achieved publication.

5
Marlborough, 1912-1913

By January 1912 Sorley had been in the Sixth Form one term. He was now at the top of the school and in a privileged position. The Sixth lived very much apart from the body of the school in a separate block of studies with their own common room. They were not so strictly bound by rules or times as the younger boys, as J.P.T. Bury's light-hearted sketch of their life shows:

> 8.20-9.0 a.m. The Hall begins to empty. The Sixth stroll across to their studies or to the form-room in the Museum Block reserved as their sanctum. A small crowd stands around the fire ready to seize on the first prefect to bring a paper across from the Hall; if it is *The Times* competition is all the keener. The *Daily Herald* makes its appearance too. In a great public school there are always many to be found ready to uphold more than liberal traditions. But the supporters of the Labour journal are not numerous. By the end of the day it would be hard to find a page of it intact. In winter its fate is usually to be fuel for the fire; in summer it would be torn and grimy on the floor or in the wastepaper basket.

Life in the Classical Sixth was not quite so leisurely as this description suggests. There was a great deal of work to be done. The emphasis being on classics, in one term Sorley had to study, among others, Plato, Tacitus and Demosthenes (whom he thought a 'short-sighted swelled-headed narrow-minded windbag'!) In French he read Victor Hugo and in English Byron. Then there was Isaiah to be studied for Divinity, Roman History (BC 280-218) and Bagehot's *English Constitution*. He was still taking maths but was allowed to drop the subject at the end of the summer term, 1912, to his great relief. 'I have found I have learnt more by giving up maths than in the whole time I did them,' he wrote to his parents, 'as instead of maths I do English with Gidney'.

A.R. Gidney, then in his early twenties, had won a double First in Greats at Corpus Christi. He replaced Atkey as Sorley's English master. Gidney's interest in literature is shown by his readiness to found a Senior Literary Society in 1910, when he had been at Marlborough only three years. There is no doubt that he was a brilliant scholar, but he was not, unfortunately, very popular as a teacher. To begin with at least he was extremely strict and seemed to the boys rather inhuman, perhaps because he tried to be entirely rational. 'Our difference about Germany,' Sorley wrote to him later, 'was the difference of people who base their opinions on sentiment and reason. I have always done the former, and let reason (such as it is) come in afterwards to provide some show of fabric'. Different as they were, they became quite fond of each other though Sorley could rarely resist poking fun at his master, whom he found slightly absurd:

> Gidney, in a fit of great kindness and rather conventional Bohemianism, [he wrote to his parents] is taking the Lit. Soc. out next Saturday to a rustic spot near by where he will feed us under an oak and celebrate the Borrow Centenary by reading us himself a paper on Borrow. The result is I am getting up Borrow for the occasion and am at present knee-deep in *Lavengro*. I like it immensely but just in the same way as you like *L'Île Inconnue*. I hardly hope to have finished it this year. Like the Bass Rock* it is very good, but always remains on the table.

The Literary Society referred to here is the Senior group, to which Sorley was transferred in October 1912 on entering the Upper Sixth. His first paper, which he read to the Society on 3 November 1912, was on John Mase-

* A famous cake.

field's trilogy—*The Everlasting Mercy*, *The Widow in the Bye Street* and *Dauber*. Masefield had replaced Meredith as Sorley's current 'deity' and was having a strong influence on his poetry at this time. His praise of Masefield shows not only his modern taste, but also the direction in which his own poetic technique was developing. For he admired Masefield's vigorous outspoken language, which marks Sorley's own work at its best:

> The voice of our poets and men of letters is finely trained and sweet to hear; it teems with sharp saws and rich sentiment, it is a marvel of delicate technique: it pleases, it flatters, it charms, it soothes: it is a living lie. The voice of John Masefield rings rough and ill-trained: it tells a story, it leaves the thinking to the reader, it gives him no dessert of sentiment, cut, dried—and ready made to go to sleep on: it jars, it grates, it makes him wonder; it is full of hope and faith and power and strife and God.

The confident and slightly didactic tone of this passage suggests that Sorley was enjoying his position of authority in the Sixth and for a moment losing something of his diffidence. It must be remembered, however, that he was just becoming aware of his literary powers and not yet conscious of the dangers of over-confidence. Ironically enough, he goes on to praise Masefield for *not* being rhetorical or pretentious:

> For Masefield writes that he knows and testifies that he has seen. Throughout his poems there are lines and phrases so instinct with life, that they betoken a man who writes of what he has experienced, not of what he thinks he can imagine: who has braved the storm, who has walked in the hells, who has seen the reality of life: who does not, like Tennyson, shut off the world he has to write about, attempting to imagine shipwrecks from the sofa or battles in his bed. Com-

pare for instance *Enoch Arden* and *Dauber*' One is a
dream: the other, life.

Again, it is this sense of authenticity which Sorley desires
in his own work, and achieves at his best. Above all he
identified with Masefield's determination to write poetry
for 'the people':

> The most awfully sad thing in history is, I think, that
> poetry up till now has been mainly by and for and
> about the Upper Classes. There has been a most horribly
> mistaken idea that poetry and the praise of God must
> be written in high-falutin' language. It can be written
> in any kind of language. If it is genuine and wells up
> irresistibly, then it is great, be the wording never so
> meagre. If it is sham or a mere religious recreation, it
> is a staring profanity, be the wording never so fine
> and sonorous. All poetry is primarily praise, praise of
> God or God's works in some form or another. And
> praise only needs verbosity to cover insincerity. Is
> there anything finer, purer or sincerer in the English
> language than this in which there is not a word that
> the lowest farm-hand might not use?

The language here is again rather stilted and rhetorical
but the sentiment is deeply felt, as we shall see.

Gidney was rightly concerned that Sorley should 'not
read only such as Masefield' and insisted on lending him
Frederick Myers's *St Paul*; the best Sorley could say of
it was that he preferred it to Browning's *Dramatic Lyrics*,
'though it might be shortened'. In a further effort to
widen Sorley's taste Gidney 'foisted' Pater on him. After
Masefield's stimulating realism Pater seemed 'the dullest
and most stilted author' Sorley had ever read. He thought
it was probably a punishment 'because I do not write
essays in the Oxford manner, as Gidney loves'. Apart
from Gidney's obsession with Pater, Sorley found him a
'very stimulating teacher'. Gidney returned the admiration.

As we have seen, he showed Sorley's verse translations
to Bickersteth, who started the Junior Literary Society
mainly for the boy's benefit. And when Gidney read
Sorley's original poems he 'never had any doubt that he
was a 'genius'. It seemed to him that the work was a
direct expression of Sorley himself:

> In his poetry there is a complete absence of the
> lusciousness common to youthful verse—nor a shadow
> of the sensual anywhere. Well, that is how his person-
> ality struck me. Its quality seemed to be the quality
> of light itself—warmth, glow, brightness, purity above
> all. He enjoyed life immensely, but was the least self-
> indulgent of boys; not that he was austere or ascetic,
> as he had no need for such disciplines; he seemed to
> live with an extraordinary thrust of life, with an
> *élan vital* harmonising itself sanely and naturally in a
> due temperance of body and spirit.

There seems to be an element of wishful thinking here,
for there is no one more sensual than Sorley at times,
though there is some truth in the description as a whole.

Nevertheless Gidney, who became Sorley's housemaster
in September 1912, did not find Sorley easy to handle.
One Sunday evening Sorley came to his room to say that
he had 'cut chapel' and to demand the usual penalty—a
caning. 'I suppose,' said Gidney, trying to avoid it, 'you
mistook the time.' Sorley, who believed in truth at all
costs and had a strong sense of justice, refused to co-
operate: 'No, sir, I was on the downs and it was so
enjoyable I decided not to come back.' Gidney tried
again, but Sorley insisted on the punishment. When
Gidney refused to inflict it, Sorley protested: 'It's very
unsatisfactory, sir; you see I shan't be able to do it again.'

The Master, Dr Wynne Willson, found Sorley equally
difficult to handle. Wynne Willson had taken over from
Frank Fletcher in September 1911 and taught Sorley
classics in the Sixth. He had started as an assistant master

at Rugby, like Fletcher, then gone on to become head-master of Haileybury. The boys found him rather fussy and pedantic and did not respect him as they had Fletcher. Sorley, who was often quick to question authority, gave him some trouble to begin with, as one of his friends, A.R. Pelly, recalls:

> Wynne Willson, 'Boodle' we called him, hadn't a clue how to handle him. I have memories of Sorley refusing to be confirmed and then later agreeing to be confirm-ed on his own terms. The Master took confirmation classes in Chapel. Boys always entered by the west door, and we were not supposed to use the south door at the other end. On one occasion I remember when we were all assembled in our places like good little boys in plenty of time, with the Master in his seat, the south door suddenly opened and in walked Sorley. He strolled the full length of Chapel and reached his seat in the nick of time with the Master glaring at him. Sorley looked up, took his watch out, looked at it and held it out to prove that he was not late, and smiled at the Master who could not conceal his annoyance and fury. (*Autobiography of A. R Pelly*, unpublished)

Pelly also remembered Sorley arguing with the Master about College rules, and what punishment they did or did not allow. When the Master gave him lines, Sorley found in some old book of rules that prefects could ask to be beaten. Like Gidney, Wynne Willson refused to beat him. So Sorley refused to do any lines and escaped punishment altogether. He was fond of imitating 'Boodle', who had an unfortunate lisp: 'Vewwy good boy, fine influence, beautiful athlete, gweat help to me,' was his version of the Master's Prize Day speech. In spite of Sorley's provocative behaviour, perhaps even because of it, Wynne Willson admired and liked him greatly: 'His personality struck me at once,' he wrote later. 'His fine face and splendid head bore the stamp of intellect and individuality'. He found it 'a daily refreshment to sit opposite to [Sorley] at "Hall" and hear him talk. He was never dull or depressed. In fact a bubbling joy in life was one of his greatest charms'. For his part Sorley 'grew to like the Master very much'. He even began to appreciate Wynne Willson's somewhat pedantic humour, though this was after he had left Marlborough:

> I wrote to the Master [he told a friend] begging him to appoint a successor to F.S. P[reston] who would be guaranteed not to join the Corps. He wrote back by return of post (he writes perfectly delightful letters) that 'anticipating my imperious wish he had already appointed an entirely non-combative gentleman,' but dashed my hopes to the ground by saying 'he was a refined scholar who could yet make many runs.' One of those unfortunate persons who not content with being good athletes are good scholars as well—ah me, my heart is wae for Marlborough.

One respect in which Sorley showed his approval of people in the Sixth was to try to convert them to Masefield. 'I remember one day when I was ill in bed,' wrote Wynne Willson, 'he sent me to read one volume of [Masefield's] poems in the morning, and when I wrote him a note of appreciation, sent me another in the afternoon. Another name for his list!' He was not so successful at converting Sorley back to Browning, as Sorley explains to a friend:

> Good luck to Robert Browning as interpreted by the Master. I have on the whole less respect for Browning than I have for Paul, who was also called Saul. But that is of course entirely my loss, and, as the Master once laboriously explained to me, I must not therefore think that St Paul or Browning mind very much. Do suggest something absurdly atheistical to the Master

(as I suppose he approaches Browning from the theological and never from the literary standpoint). Browning has . . . a hearty bounding incorrigible optimism which must be very comforting to Christians. He was always content with second best.

Sorley was now openly rejecting conventional Christianity, to the distress of Wynne Willson. Despite his parents' upbringing and Professor Sorley's inability to take orders, they had become Anglicans on moving to Cambridge and sent their children to a Church of England Sunday School. Sorley had been able to accept the Church's teaching until confirmation, which, as we have seen, he initially refused. But there is no doubt that he had already begun to question conventional beliefs some time before. At Marlborough, for instance, he refused to sing hymns in Latin because he felt its use to be an affectation, but he joined in lustily with those he felt rang true. He was very critical of conventional or commonplace sermons, though he listened intently to thoughtful ones. He judged clergymen on their own merits, admiring those who were intelligent and scorning those who were not. He rejected conventions in religion, as he rejected them in poetry, when he could not see their relevance to his own life and work. His earliest poems show that he was beginning to find more meaning in nature than in church and his attraction towards the wilder aspects of nature give his beliefs an almost pagan aspect, which remind us of his Celtic origin:

> I do not know if it seems brave
> The youthful spirit to enslave,
> And hedge about, lest it should grow.
> I don't know if it's better so
> In the long end. I only know
> That when I have a son of mine,
> He shan't be made to droop and pine,
> Bound down and forced by rule and rod

To serve a God who is no God.
But I'll put custom on the shelf
And make him find his God himself.
Perhaps he'll find him in a tree,
Some hollow trunk, where you can see.
Perhaps the daisies in the sod
Will open out and show him God.
Or will he meet him in the roar
Of breakers as they beat the shore?
Or in the spiky stars that shine?
Or in the rain (where I found mine)? — ('What You Will')

Sorley feels that conventional religion is so often 'self-conscious' and 'other-worldly', which is another reason he turns to nature:

> Oak and beech and birch,
> Like a church, but homelier than church,
> The black trunks for its walls of tile;
> Its roof, old leaves; its floor, beech nuts;
> The squirrels its congregation—

'The Other Wise Man', from which this extract is taken, tells the story of a fourth Wise Man, who decided to leave the other three and go his own way. In all probability this is Sorley's own declaration of independence in religious matters. 'The earth even more than Christ,' he declares, 'is the ultimate ideal of what man should strive to be.' As with his poetry, it is the bleak Marlborough downs which have inspired him:

> ' . . . Heed not what the preachers say
> Of a good land far away.
> Here's a better land and kind
> And it is not far to find.'

> Therefore, when we rise and sing
> Of a distant land, so fine,
> Where the bells for ever ring,
> And the suns for ever shine:

Singing loud and singing grand,
Of a happy far-off land,
O! I smile to hear the song,
For I know that they are wrong,
That the happy land and gay
Is not very far away,
And that I can get there soon
Any rainy afternoon.

And when summer comes again,
And the downs are dimpling green,
And the air is free from rain,
And the clouds no longer seen:
Then I know that they have gone
To find a new camp further on,
Where there is no shining sun
To throw light on what is done,
Where the summer can't intrude
On the fort where winter stood:
  —Only blown and drenching grasses,
  Only rain that never passes,
  Moving mists and sweeping wind,
  And I follow them behind!

— ('Rain')

In spite of his rejection of orthodox Christianity—'a casual heretic' Wynne Willson called him—there is no doubt that Sorley was deeply religious. He was constantly searching for a meaning in life, and found it eventually in a spiritual, rather than a materialistic realm. His attitude towards life was reverential, though never priggish. It is significant that the Church of England have taken one of his poems, 'Expectans Expectavi', and turned it into an anthem:

From morn to midnight, all day through,
I laugh and play as others do,
I sin and chatter, just the same
As others with a different name.

And all year long upon the stage
I dance and tumble and do rage
So vehemently, I scarcely see
The inner and eternal me.

I have a temple I do not
Visit, a heart I have forgot,
A self that I have never met,
A secret shrine—and yet, and yet

This sanctuary of my soul
Unwitting I keep white and whole,
Unlatched and lit, if Thou should'st care
To enter or to tarry there.

With parted lips and outstretched hands
And listening ears Thy servant stands.
Call Thou early, call Thou late,
To Thy great service dedicate.

This poem is something of an enigma since it is dated May 1915 by Sorley's father in his scholarly editions of his son's poetry. However, it is undated in the original MS and it is quite clear both from its content and technique that it could not possibly have been written later than the end of 1913. Sorley is unlikely to have used the phrases 'laugh and play' and 'sin and chatter' of himself in wartime France. He is even more unlikely to have used the conventionally religious language of the last three stanzas later than December 1913 when he quite deliberately rejects organised religion in 'The Other Wise Man'. 'Expectans Expectavi' is much closer in tone, content and technique to 'Peace', published in December 1912 and 'The Seekers', published in March 1913.

Sorley's rejection of orthodox religion occurred at the height of his rebellion against the conventions of public school life. This rebellion showed itself most clearly in his work, as Wynne Willson records:

He had the makings of a good pure classical scholar, but he revolted against the routine of classical education and vowed that he would not read for 'Mods' at Oxford. In the VIth we were reading Martial one term. Something in this writer (probably his subservience and smug deference) stirred the boy's wrath. Nothing would induce him to work at the author ... But we came to some kind of working agreement. He did a modicum at work he disliked, and threw himself heart and soul into anything that touched humanity and reality.

Sorley's mother believed that he 'found freedom' in these last two years at school and what descriptions we have of him seem to prove her right. On one of the family visits to Marlborough he asked his parents if they had read Masefield's *The Widow in the Bye Street*, which was thought rather shocking at that time. When they replied that they had, but that it had been 'chained up from the youth of the flock', he could not conceal his scorn: 'I've bought a copy and am lending it to people.' His sister felt that Marlborough had made more of a 'gentleman' of him and that 'his manners both physical and verbal developed a certain *élan*. They became grandiose—to give pleasure and to amuse, *not* out of arrogance.' One of her memories suggests that he had certainly become more urbane. He had been invited in the holidays to an engagement party given by a Mrs Crae, for her daughter. Sorley was introduced to the daughter and danced with her, 'chatting and behaving with his new-found vivacity and social charm'. When he led her back to her seat at the end of the dance, she was immediately claimed by her fiancé, a Dr Roderick, who completely ignored Sorley. 'Charles, very adult, remarked "That man Roderick is the sort of man I can't stand".' Sorley himself gives us a glimpse into his life as a Sixthformer in the fourth section of 'A Call to Action', which has never before been published:

Soon after lunch we take a chair,
   And light a comforting cigar,
And muse with languid, mild, despair
   Upon the state in which things are.

The shadows lengthen on the wall,
   The evening chill pervades the air;
We may have been asleep—at all
   Events we are still sitting there!

Sorley, who had been made a prefect and house captain, was now one of the leading lights at Marlborough. Beside reading papers to the Senior Literary Society, he made witty speeches at the Debating Society and helped re-form the Dramatic Society. It was no wonder that he himself now became a 'demigod' to the younger boys in his house. Arthur Pelly, for instance, thought him 'a great character' and Alan Hutchinson and Cecil Harvey continued to write to him long after he had left the school. Sorley was not comfortable in this position of lofty superiority and tried to put these relationships on a more equal footing as soon as possible. He regarded prefectship as a 'prison-house' and felt that such 'artificial positions of responsibility' were 'a poison to the character of those who hold them'. 'Pity poor prefects!' he warned his young friend Harvey. 'You have to act from day to day and say what you don't think in dormitory and think that you are good and become a prig. It has ruined many people'. But prefectship could not ruin Sorley, who was far too self-critical to allow of any strong sense of self-importance. He admitted his 'deficiency in squashing power', but this only made him even more popular with the boys. Francis Turner, who was in Sorley's dormitory in C_1, remembers how kind he was to the younger boys: 'He was a competent, but not particularly strict head of dormitory and prefect—he had no need to be, since we all liked him so much we did what he told us without trouble'.

In spite of his popularity, Sorley became increasingly critical of Marlborough. It was precisely this popularity that worried him:

When one reaches the top of a public school, one has such unbounded opportunities of getting unbearably conceited that I don't see how anyone survives the change that must come when the tin god is swept off his little kingdom and becomes an unimportant mortal again. And besides I am sure it is far too enjoyable, and one is awfully tempted to pose all the time and be theatrical.

Sorley felt that public schools were 'run on the worn-out fallacy that there can't be progress without competition'. He thought that 'people of a certain type' should not be allowed to stay on too long; in fact, if he were the Master, he would superannuate the successes, not the failures. Once again we find him sympathising with what he calls the 'obadiah-stick-in-the-mires' and almost apologetic about his own success, which he feels is corrupting. He hates the way the 'public school atmosphere develops the nasty tyrannical instincts' and he despises the hierarchical system, where prefects and athletes become gods. Advising his young friend Hutchinson about a choice of books for a prize, he writes:

To begin with, it is unnecessary to have them bound. I have always thought that the way they insisted on having all books bound was eminently typical of the public school attitude to life and humanity: 'spend more than half always on exteriors; as long as the outside is nice and showy, Lord! what do the contents and kernel matter?'

The contents and kernel mattered very much to Sorley, who also needed to feel related to the outside world. He particularly disliked learning classics because they seemed to him so removed from reality, as he saw it at this time. For his thoughts were turning more and more to the underprivileged and socially deprived. This was partly as a reaction to the privileged world of the public school, partly because he had come into contact with Alexander Paterson, a well-known social reformer of the day. In the Lent term of 1911 Sorley had heard Paterson speak: 'It was a magnificent lecture,' he wrote to his parents; 'I have never heard a better: he was humorous and practical and had no nonsense or cant or missionary canvassing about him'. When he read Paterson's *Across the Bridges* the following term his enthusiasm for Paterson's theories grew. He secretly determined to devote himself to the same cause and 'become an instructor in a Working Man's College or something of that sort'. Masefield, as we have seen, sharpened his interest in the working classes. So that when his dissatisfaction with public school life reached its peak and he had grown 'utterly satiated by the artificiality of the atmosphere' he suddenly decided in January 1913 that he must leave Marlborough to become an Elementary School teacher. This idea had been precipitated by an argument with Atkey, who had been naturally most upset by Sorley's desire to give up classics. But it was not until Atkey's friend Dyson, the music-master, stepped in that Sorley gave way. George Dyson, who later became Sir George and head of the Royal College of Music, was quite different from most of the masters Sorley had encountered at Marlborough. For he had had neither a public school, nor Oxbridge education. This immediately won Sorley's approval: 'A man like Dyson,' he told Hutchinson, 'without a public school education and a mind that never curled itself up, but was always ready to receive new things was invaluable at Marlborough'. Dyson won the boys over with his blunt north-country approach to teaching and they learnt eagerly under him. He became a close friend of Sorley's other two favourites, Bickersteth and Atkey. When Dyson left in 1914 Sorley lamented:

'If the last of the trio—Atkey—also leaves, there's an end of Marlborough'. Dyson, who had done some social work himself, knew how to handle Sorley. He pointed out that Sorley's decision to leave would defeat its own end and that the only way to get the kind of career he wished was to keep on with classics and go to university—'merely as a means to an end'. He would then be able to get his post at a night-school or working-man's college without difficulty. Sorley was particularly impressed by Dyson's final point:

> While up at Oxford, he showed me, I could make a beginning by working at Oxford House, and, after I had got a scholarship, there would be no pressing need to continue those detestable Classics in the detestably serious spirit demanded. I could spend a lot of time in social work and make a beginning then.

Sorley found the prospect of another year of being 'a little tin god' at Marlborough 'alarmingly and disastrously alluring'. It was precisely because he loved it so much and wanted to stay on that he had decided to leave. But on the whole he thought Dyson's advice sound and was extremely grateful—'if ever I forget the kindness of Dyson, I ought to be knocked down'.

Sorley now settled down to work for a scholarship to Oxford. From being second and first respectively in his first two terms in the Lower Sixth, he had slipped right down to twenty-second (out of twenty-three) when he moved to the Upper Sixth in September 1912. Having decided to stay with a specific purpose in mind, his results improved again, to thirteenth and fifteenth respectively, but it was not until Michaelmas 1913, when he took his scholarship, that he showed what he could do when he applied himself. From fifteenth he rose to fifth in form, had three pieces of work specially commended, won the senior Farrar Prize for English Literature and Language, the Buchanan Prize for Public Reading and gained a scholarship to University College, Oxford.

At games, too, he was more successful. From being in the House Rugger XV in 1912 he ascended to the dizzy heights of the School 2nd XV in Michaelmas 1913: 'I suppose you would be angry if I concealed the fact that I have got a "forty" cap,' he wrote to his parents, 'which, being interpreted, is about the same as a second XV'.[1]

Sorley now felt like the boy in the 'Success' section of his poem 'A Tale of Two Careers', which he had written the year before:

> He does not dress as other men,
>   His 'kish'[2] is loud and gay,
> His 'side'[3] is as the 'side' of ten
>   Because his 'barnes'[4] are grey.
>
> His head has swollen to a size
>   Beyond the proper size for heads,
> He metaphorically buys
>   The ground on which he treads.
>
> Before his face of haughty grace
>   The ordinary mortal cowers:
> A 'forty-cap' has put the chap
>   Into another world from ours.

Sorley is obviously amused by the effects of success, but he is still saddened by the fate of the failures, to whom he devotes the second section of the poem:

> We are the wasters, who have no
>   Hope in this world here, neither fame,
> Because we cannot collar low[5]

[1] Marlborough rugger teams were originally composed of twenty players a side.

[2] 'Kish': a folding cushion in which the boys also carried their books.

[3] 'Side': assumption of superiority.

[4] 'Barnes': the grey flannel trousers worn by 'bloods'.

[5] 'Collar low': a term meaning to tackle or lay hold of and stop an opponent in football who is holding the ball.

> Nor write a strange dead tongue the same
> As strange dead men did long ago.

Sorley reflected on such problems while he rambled across the downs alone, for he loved walking more than ever. At the end of the Lent term, 1912, he had walked home, over a hundred miles from Marlborough to Cambridge. His mother has given us a sketch of his four-day trip:

> It was stipulated that he should spend the nights in a bed under cover, and not under hedge or haystack as he proposed; but there are evidences that the condition—if there was one—was not taken too seriously by him. Part of his way lay along the bank of the canal by Hungerford; here he found the dead straight line of the tow-path so unbearable that, to keep going at all, he had to repeat aloud the thirty-fifth chapter of Isaiah,[1] which he had just learned as an imposition. He gaily told his first teacher [i.e. Mrs Sorley] that it was the only portion of the Bible which he could remember by heart.

In September 1913 Sorley walked back to school from Fenny Stratford and his spirits rose as he approached the downs again:

> The last day was the best of all. Almost all the time I was seven or eight hundred feet up, for I was walking on the ridge that forms the southern wall of the White Horse Vale, and all the time had a fine panorama to my right. The early morning was thick with mist, but cleared up wonderfully later on. There was a track all the way, sufficiently visible to follow, and I kept it till the ridge breaks off due south of Swindon. Then I turned at right angles on to the top of that other ridge that runs by east of the road from Swindon to

[1] 'The wilderness and the solitary place shall be glad for them; . . .'

Marlborough, and separates Wilts and Berks, and on its back I threaded my way back to College.

For Sorley the downs were full of mysterious meaning. Where other people saw hillocks, he saw ancient Roman camps, where his family saw merely a field covered with white stones, he 'stared at the field as if he saw something written on it'. And he did:

> This field is almost white with stones
>   That cumber all its thirsty crust.
> And underneath, I know, are bones,
>   And all around is death and dust.
>
> And if you love a livelier hue—
>   O, if you love the youth of year,
> When all is clean and green and new,
>   Depart. There is no summer here.
>
> Albeit, to me there lingers yet
>   In this forbidding stony dress
> The impotent and dim regret
>   For some forgotten restlessness.
>
> Dumb, imperceptibly astir,
>   These relics of an ancient race,
> These men, in whom the dead bones were
>   Still fortifying their resting-place. ('Stones')

As we have seen, the downs were Sorley's main source of inspiration at Marlborough. However, his first poems, which started to appear in the *Marlburian* in July 1912, were concerned more with school life and are often no more than clever doggerel. This is true of at least the first four—'Verses for C_1 House Concert', 'The Massacre' ('a rendering, in verse, of a dream of the author's after a somewhat extravagant meal, for the details and sentiments of which he does not hold himself responsible'), 'A Tale of Two Careers' and 'A Call to Action'. The last two are more serious in content, 'A Tale of Two Careers' being concerned with success and failure in public schools and 'A Call to Action' another outburst against school-life:

> We preach and prattle, peer and pry
>   And fit together two and two:
> We ponder, argue, shout, swear, lie —
>   We will not, for we cannot, DO.
>
> Pale puny soldiers of the pen,
>   Absorbed in this your inky strife,
> Act as of old, when men were men,
>   England herself and life yet life.

In the fifth and hitherto unpublished section of this poem Sorley concludes half-humorously, half-seriously— with social work in mind, no doubt:

> We must be taught to Act: 'tis vain
>   To tear the hair and beat the brow,
> Wring dry the thoughts, ransack the brain
>   And write — as I am doing now!

Yet he continued to write and his next four poems, which appeared in the *Marlburian* between November 1912 and February 1913, show more technical skill and less facetiousness, though they are still obviously apprentice work. 'Rain', the first of these four, has already been quoted as proof of Sorley's rejection of conventional religion and his mystical belief in the power behind the wilder elements of Nature:

> —Only blown and drenching grasses,
> Only rain that never passes,
> Moving mists and sweeping wind,
> And I follow them behind.

In 'Peace' Sorley seems to be experimenting with different rhythms, few of them original. It is hard not to think of Rudyard Kipling's 'Mandalay', John Masefield's 'Ships' and 'John Brown's Body' when reading the opening stanzas:

There is silence in the evening when the long days cease,
And a million men are praying for an ultimate release
From strife and sweat and sorrow—they are praying
                                        for peace.
      But God is marching on.

Peace for a people that is striving to be free!
Peace for the children of the wild wet sea!
Peace for the seekers of the promised land—do we
      Want peace when God has none?

The most interesting aspect of this poem is the conflict it reflects in Sorley between a desire to luxuriate in poetry and a feeling that it is his duty to *act*, for the benefit of mankind. It is a recurring theme in the early poetry and one which is related to his decision to give up the 'unrealities' of classics for social work in the East End of London. The conflict was probably provoked by the rather dismissive attitude towards poetry to be found in most public schools of his day, partly by heredity. For the shadow of a Calvinistic grandfather hovers over the early work:

If you want to know the beauty of the thing called rest,
Go, get it from the poets, who will tell you it is best
(And their words are sweet as honey) to lie flat
                       upon your chest
      And sleep till life is gone.

I know that there is beauty where the low streams run,
And the weeping of the willows and the big sunk sun,
But I know my work is doing and it never shall be done,
      Though I march for ages on.

In 'The River', which is based on an actual case of suicide, Sorley allows himself to luxuriate in words and rhythms.

97

The mood of the poem reminds one of Dowson's 'Spleen'
and Wilde's 'Ballad of Reading Gaol', while the technique
is reminiscent of Coleridge's 'Ancient Mariner'. In spite
of its derivativeness and some padding it impresses by
its skilful use of rhyme (every alternate line rhymes with
'sky' throughout) and by its strange insights into an un-
balanced mind:

> . . . It was not that the man had sinned,
>   Or that he wished to die.
> Only the wide and silent tide
>   Went slowly sweeping by.
>
> The mass of blackness moving down
>   Filled full of dreams the eye;
> The lights of all the lighted town
>   Ypon its breast did lie;
> The tall black trees were upside down
>   In the river's phantasy.
>
> He had an envy for its black
>   Inscrutability;
> He felt impatiently the lack
>   Of that great law whereby
> The river never travels back
>   But still goes gliding by;
>
> But still goes gliding by, nor clings
>   To passing things that die,
> Nor shows the secrets that it brings
>   From its strange source on high.
> And he felt 'We are two living things
>   And the weaker one is I.'
>
>   *   *   *   *
>
> He had a yearning for the strength
>   That comes of unity:
> The union of one soul at length
>   With its twin-soul to lie:

To be a part of one great strength
That moves and cannot die. . . .

'The Seekers', though expressing very worthwhile sentiments, is marred by the same piousness which spoilt 'Peace'. In it Sorley swings back to a resolve to devote himself to good works, for his sympathies are all with 'the publican and harlot', the 'spurned', the 'fool', the 'sinner', the 'scorned and rejected', the 'afflicted, destitute and weak'.

The subject matter of 'What You Will', which follows in June 1913, is less clichéd. Here, as we have seen,[1] Sorley criticises the enslavement of the young by rules and conventions, suggesting that they should be allowed to go their own way and find their own truth in life. But the verse is still rather clumsy and it is not until we come to his two versions of 'Rooks' that we find him matching maturity of thought with a more skilful technique and some striking imagery:

> There, where the rusty iron lies,[2]
>   The rooks are cawing all the day.
> Perhaps no man, until he dies,
>   Will understand them, what they say.
>
> The evening makes the sky like clay.
>   The slow wind waits for night to rise.
> The world is half-content. But they
>
> Still trouble all the trees with cries,
>   That know, and cannot put away,
> The yearning to the soul that flies
>   From day to night, from night to day.

[1] See pages 61 and 84-85.

[2] The rookery at Marlborough College was in the trees standing between C House garden and the bathing place. Under these trees a great deal of rubbish used to be thrown, among it rusty iron. Sorley would have been able to see the rookery from his dormitory window.

Written on two rhymes throughout this poem has an
unusual stanza form of 4 lines, 3 lines, 4 lines, which
draws the reader to the centre of the poem then leads
him out again to the conclusion, where the poet's soul
and the birds are mysteriously unified. The colour of the
evening sky is brilliantly captured in the image of red
unbaked clay. Sorley may have been dissatisfied with
the padding in the fourth line of this poem and the
slight obscurity of the last stanza, for he produced another
version of 'Rooks' a few weeks later. In it he expresses
his mystical sense of oneness with the birds more effectively and his belief that his poetry and the birds' cry are
both an expression of something 'Strange and unsatisfied
and sweet'. It is significant that Sorley, who preferred
rain and wind to sun, should find the ugly cawing of the
rooks 'sweet'. Once more we are reminded of a primitive,
pagan streak in him, not of the comfortable twentieth
century, but perhaps related to his Calvinistic forbears.
Sorley continues to experiment this time choosing a five
line stanza with an ababb rhyme scheme. The need to
find three rhymes in one verse leads him to pad occasionally, though he allows himself to use half-rhymes. The
imagery is predominantly biblical, almost certainly to
lend weight to his musings on immortality:

> . . . Yet how? since everything must pass
> At evening with the sinking sun,
> And Christ is gone, and Barabbas,
> Judas and Jesus, gone, clean gone,
> Then how shall I live on?
>
> Yet surely Judas must have heard
> Amidst his torments the long cry
> Of some lone Israelitish bird,
> And on it, ere he came to die,
> Thrown all his spirit's agony.

And that immortal cry which welled
 For Judas, ever afterwards
Passion on passion still has swelled
 And sweetened: so to-night these birds
 Will take my words, will take my words.

And wrapping them in music meet
 Will sing their spirit through the sky,
Starnge and unsatisfied and sweet:
 That, when stock-dead am I, am I,
 O, that can never die!

'Stones', written in July 1913, the same month as
'Rooks (II)', shows an amazing leap forward in technical
ability. Perhaps it is because Sorley has found a subject
entirely congenial to his austere outlook in this description
of an ancient race evoked for him by the white stones.
These, as we have seen,[1] are symbolic of the dead men's
bones, but also of their hard hearts and barren lives:

Their field of life was white with stones;
 Good fruit to earth they never brought.
O, in these bleached and buried bones
 Was neither love nor faith nor thought.

But like the wind in this bleak place,
 Bitter and bleak and sharp they grew,
And bitterly they ran their race,
 A brutal, bad, unkindly crew:

Souls like the dry earth, hearts like stone,
 Brains like that barren bramble-tree:
Stern, sterile, senseless, mute, unknown—
 But bold, O, bolder far than we!

This is Sorley's own voice. The language is direct, save
for a few archaisms. The imagery is equally straightforward, being taken either from nature or the Bible.
The stanza form is also simple but effective and the

[1] See page 95.

tone brooding, sometimes nostalgic, though never pessimistic. The thought is unusual for a youth of eighteen: even primitive man, Sorley argues, had something to redeem him—a boldness which has gone from modern life, leaving it flabby and undemanding.

The theme is repeated in 'Barbury Camp', another evocation of the past, this time inspired by the pre-Roman fortifications of that name on the Marlborough downs. Sorley relates the primitive power of the men who built the camp to their worship of the wind and rain, which, as we know, he shared:

> We burrowed night and day with tools of lead,
> Heaped the bank up and cast it in a ring
> And hurled the earth above. And Caesar said,
> 'Why, it is excellent. I like the thing.'
> We, who are dead,
> Made it, and wrought, and Caesar liked the thing.
>
> And here we strove, and here we felt each vein
> Ice-bound, each limb fast frozen, all night long.
> And here we held communion with the rain
> That lashed as into manhood with its thong,
> Cleansing through pain.
> And the wind visited us and made us strong.

The stanza form is more complex than usual, with a short penultimate line for emphasis. Emphasis is also achieved through a deliberate use of repetition, strong rhythms and almost childishly simple language. Rejecting the Christian dichotomy between love and hate, good and evil, heaven and hell, Sorley suggests that both must be embraced in a much fiercer attitude towards life and death:

> So, fighting men and winds and tempests, hot
> With joy and hate and battle-lust, we fell
> Where we fought. And God said, 'Killed at last then? What!

Ye that are too strong for heaven, too clean for hell,
(God said) stir not.
This be your heaven, or, if ye will, your hell.'

Sorley, who reminded a friend that his name was Gaelic
for 'wanderer', was attracted by restlessness and cease-
less action: 'Give me the Odyssey and I return the New
Testament to store,' he wrote to the same friend. He is
a pagan at heart:

So again we fight and wrestle, and again
Hurl the earth up and cast it in a ring.
But when the wind comes up, driving the rain
(Each rain-drop a fiery steed), and the mists rolling
Up from the plain,
This wild procession, this impetuous thing,

Hold us amazed. We mount the wind-cars, then
Whip up the steeds and drive through all the world,
Searching to find somewhere some brethren,
Sons of the winds and waters of the world.
We, who were men,
Have sought, and found no men in all this world.

Wind, that has blown here always ceaselessly,
Bringing, if any man can understand,
Might to the mighty, freedom to the free;
Wind, that has caught us, cleansed us, made us grand,
Wind that is we
(We that were men)—make men in all this land,

That so may live and wrestle and hate that when
They fall at last exultant, as we fell,
And come to God, God may say, 'Do you come then
Mildly enquiring, is it heaven or hell?
Why! Ye were men!
Back to your winds and rains. Be these your heaven
and hell!'

Sorley is at his most original so far in these poems

about the elemental power of nature. He is more deriv-
ative when he tries to describe her gentler aspects, as in
'Autumn Dawn' and 'East Kennet Church at Evening'.
Sorley himself admits that 'Autumn Dawn' had too
much copy from Meredith in it, though he makes good
use of it to draw a contrast between two moods of
nature at dawn. The difference between the heavy leth-
argic greyness of one —

> And this is morning. Would you think
> That this was the morning, when the land
> Is full of heavy eyes that blink
> Half-opened, and the tall trees stand
> Too tired to shake away the drops
> Of passing night that cling around
> Their branches and weigh down their tops:
> And the grey sky leans on the ground?

and the sparkling gaiety of the other mood —

> . . . The earth has eyes,
> The earth has voice, the earth has breath,
> As o'er the land and through the air,
> With wingéd sandals, Life and Death
> Speed hand in hand — that winsome pair!

is brought out by the handling of the diction and the
octysyllabic metre, which show his increasing technical
skill.

Sorley wrote 'Autumn Dawn' on his walk back to
Marlborough in September 1913,[1] but his feeling for the
countryside is expressed more simply and effectively in
a poem written on the same occasion—'Return'—despite
echoes from Rupert Brooke's 'Granchester':

> Still stand the downs so wise and wide?
> Still shake the trees their tresses grey?
> I thought their beauty might have died
> Since I had been away.

[1] See pages 94-95.

I might have known the things I love,
 The winds, the flocking birds' full cry,
The trees that toss, the downs that move,
 Were longer things than I . . .

Sorley's 'Return' in September 1913 was his last. For in December, with a scholarship to University College, Oxford, safely gained and two terms of leisure to look forward to, he suddenly decided to leave. His reasons were complex. He found 'the surroundings of Marlborough and one or two of the inhabitants . . . almost un-do-without-able', but he could 'not endure the position of Head of the House any longer':

> I had a dreadful warning at the beginning of the term when I talked public-school-story rot instead of refusing to make a mountain from a mole-hill, and preached a sermon instead of bursting out laughing. I couldn't risk degrading myself again, in case ——— tried a similar joke a second time: but in such a position it is almost impossible not to.

Before the corrupting effects of power got worse, Sorley felt he must leave. 'Public school life is after all only a rehearsal' he argued and he preferred the 'real thing to the rehearsal'. Gidney, who had grown increasingly attached to him, reacted violently to his decision and tried hard to prevent him leaving. Sorley begged his father to 'disregard Gidney's sermons' and Professor Sorley did so. He and Mrs Sorley felt that it would be good for their son to have several months abroad 'as a break between the grooves of public school and university'.

It cost Sorley a great deal to give up a further six months in his beloved Marlborough countryside and the few close friends he had made at school. In theory he despised the public school system, but he was forced to confess that it had given him 'five years that could hardly have been more enjoyable'. There seems something al-

most masochistic in his decision to deprive himself of all
he loved best; perhaps it was his Calvinistic heritage
showing itself again. Life at Marlborough was too pleasant
and too comfortable and not challenging enough, therefore he must leave it before he became smug and
self-satisfied. As it was, he felt that his reaction to
leaving was that of 'an egoist, sentimentalist, or poser':
'I regarded it,' he told Hutchinson, 'from a purely
personal standpoint and considered it a great tragedy,
having a lamentable lack of perspective'.

The last night of term was the worst and, as he strug-
gled miserably 'with innumerable packing-cases in the
void of an empty, swept and garnished study', he tried to
put things in perspective by reminding himself, humor-
ously, of the disappointment he had felt at Marlborough:

> It was spring. And we hoped in the spring
>   For a glorious summer.
> And the summer came, yes, good old thing!
>   But we found the newcomer
>
> Was bright but in days of hope gone,
>   But approaching (poor harlot)
> Threw us tattered raiment to don
>   And gave others the scarlet.
>
> So this is the end of it all!
>   Of the sloth and the slumber,
> Of the hates that we hated like gall,
>   And the loves, few in number.
>
> And no one will now Pity say
>   Or can back again wish us,
> Who have done nothing good in our day,
>   And (what's worse) nothing vicious.
>
> We have fought for ourselves like black Hell,
>   But, since we were our standard,
> Does it matter we have not fought well
>   And weak failed where we planned hard?

The time made us Outcast and Dunce,
  Though for Kingship intended.
It might have been beautiful--once!
  But now it is ended.

As this poem and other evidence show it was not the college Sorley feared leaving:

. . . for Marlborough to me [he told Hutchinson] means the 'little red-capped town' (sorry for quoting from myself!) and the land that shelters it: not the school which has given it so much and so transient notoriety. It is absurd to say that the school means one's friends there and therefore one should wish to be labelled O[ld] M[arlburian]. The bulk of the people one meets at school are shadowy substances, partially detaching themselves from the huge artificial mass Marlburian and soon disappearing again thereinto. One's (few) friends have a value entirely apart from the accidental circumstances which brought one together with them.

Sorley tried for a long time to express 'the impression that the land north of Marlborough must leave on all those whose minds' wheels are not clogged and the motive power of their mind not diverted by the artificial machinations that go on within the College Gates'. It was not until he thought of an old sign-post which pointed across the downs to Ogbourne, Marlborough, Mildenhall snd Aldbourne and forced himself to describe it as simply as possible that he felt he had succeeded in conveying what Marlborough meant to him:

LOST

Across my past imaginings
  Has dropped a blindness silent and slow,
My eye is bent on other things
  Than those it once did see and know.

I may not think on those dear lands
  (O far away and long ago!)
Where the old battered sign-post stands,
  And silently the four roads go.

East, west, south and north,
  And the cold winter winds do blow.
And what the evening will bring forth
  Is not for me nor you to know.

As Sorley himself points out: 'Simplicity, paucity of words, monotony almost, and mystery are necessary' here and these are the qualities which distinguish his best poetry of this first period.

6
Schwerin

At Schwerin in Mecklenburg Sorley discovered a language and a people. He also experienced for the first time the pleasures of independence. It was as a person rather than a poet that he developed, though there is a noticeable increase in the maturity of his work afterwards.

Germany had been chosen for Sorley by his parents mainly because Professor Sorley had enjoyed two summers at Tübingen and Berlin as a student. Before sending his son to a German university, however, he thought it necessary for him to improve his knowledge of the language. After some enquiries he chose the quiet provincial town of Schwerin in northern Germany, a place, according to Mrs Sorley 'where people still said grace before meat, and meant it'. The family chosen was equally safe—a lawyer, Herr Doktor Beutin, and his wife who was to give Charles lessons.[1]

Sorley, who had never attended very carefully in his German classes at school, made a desperate attempt to brush it up before meeting the Beutins. 'I am writing this letter in the intervals of weeping over Beresford Webb's German Grammar,' he told Hutchinson on 4 January 1914. 'The only three complimentary adjectives he has yet introduced—to set against pages of tired, sick, idle, old, bad-tempered aunts who eat stale bread, use blunt knives and everlastingly are losing them—the only nice adjectives are very begrudging and left-handed—"pious", "industrious" and "amiable". And Lord! it is always the Count who is pious and the landlord who is amiable and Charles who is industrious. And can you, I ask you, imagine three more irreconcilable and impossible states of affairs?' He was, therefore, rather apprehensive

---

[1] In his edition of Charles's letters Professor Sorley called them Bieder, to hide their identity.

about the natives when he set off for Germany on 20 January. But even before reaching Schwerin he realized that Beresford Webb was unreliable from several points of view. Not only did Sorley find his 'fluent racy and idiomatic German' completely unintelligible to the people and theirs to him; he also discovered that the Germans were far from gloomy, as the grammarian had led him to expect. Mrs Sorley, who was convinced he would die of cold in Germany, had filled many cases with warm clothes and this 'so viel Gepäck' amused the ticket-collector on the Hagenow train greatly: 'so much so that he brought another official to see me,' Sorley reported home, 'and they both made jokes (which I did not understand) and I laughed enormously and said "ah ja" in the intervals of laughter'.

The Germans were also very kind, as Sorley discovered when he found his black trunk missing at Hamburg. For he was immediately reassured by a Thomas Cook interpreter, who also deposited his remaining luggage for him and showed him the platform for his next train. Sorley was so impressed that he 'gave him one and six and left the station at once', contrary to instructions. When he eventually reached the Beutins' flat in Schwerin, it was to find that they had gone to the station to meet him—another proof of German kindness, he felt.

This first impression was strengthened by their welcome, which was noisy and good-humoured, and by their appearance, as he tells his parents:

> Dr B. is a tall fat hearty man with moustaches. If he was English he might be a bounder, but being a German he is perfectly delightful. . . . The Frau is nice-looking, smaller, and not stout: indeed she drinks no milk (I learnt this morning) for she trembles to become thick. She is very simple and delightful and knows English quite well. She is going to give me stunden.[1]

[1] Stunden: lessons.

The Neuphilolog[1] did not appear till Abendessen.[2] He is thin, fair, and pale, with pince-nez and a nervous manner. He is like most booksellers' assistants to behold. Frau B. immediately told me in his presence that he was a "Bücherwurm" and he seemed to glory in the title. Apparently, like the too hasty widower of Bowes, "they tax him" about it. He knows no English to speak of and is very eager to be kind.

During supper Sorley realized how simple and affectionate the family were, with their unashamed love of food and their horseplay round the table—'[they] slap each other's cheeks continually'. He was also given a demonstration of the Herr Doktor's musical abilities at the harmonium, for which he thanked him profusely, little realizing how weary he would grow of such performances. 'Their one idea,' he concludes in his first letter home, 'is that I should be "zufrieden",[3] and though they cannot reconcile this with my sleeping with an open window, they ensured it by offering me and allowing me a hot bath . . . and by numerous other attentions'.

Sorley enjoyed being treated as an adult. For the first time in his life he had a room to himself with 'a bed of decent length, and a washstand, a wardrobe, two tables and plenty of room besides'. After a Marlborough dormitory it seemed 'all that could be desired' and on his first morning in Schwerin he lay in bed till eleven, luxuriating in his new-found freedom. He quickly joined in with the Beutins' routine, however, eating what they called 'first' breakfast at 8.30, 'second' breakfast at noon, the main meal of the day at 4 p.m. and a light meal at eight. There were daily lessons with the Frau and skating with her brother, 'who always tumbles when

[1] Neuphilolog: first-year university student. He was Frau Beutin's brother.

[2] Abendessen: the evening meal (which was not the main meal of the day, but more like supper.

[3] Zufrieden: contented, satisfied.

he skates and prefers going softly, like me and Hezekiah'. And when the ice melted he could start exploring the surrounding countryside. His first impression had been unfavourable: 'It is chiefly when I look out over this bare and arable landscape here that I damn myself for leaving,' he wrote home: 'for after all it is the surrounding country that makes M.C., and the surroundings of Marlborough have a strangely attractive property'. Very soon, 'in spite of a patriotic determination to resist all temptations towards favourable criticism', he became reconciled to the difference and began to find the Mecklenburg landscape 'quite beautiful':

> more than that, walking is not, as I had feared, confined to main roads, but there are innumerable cross-country tracks, and the word 'verboten'[1] very seldom defiles the landscape. The country is inclined to be flat, but there are several little hills from which the view of Schwerin is not so ugly as on the post-cards I sent to the maids. So far, on each of my walks, I have found two new lakes, of which one is probably really new: and the country round is remarkably uninhabited, so altogether I'm not complaining.

Sorley became even more reconciled to leaving Marlborough when he discovered the Schwerin Hockey Club, which he promptly joined. 'I hope you will not think me ungrateful,' he wrote to Wynne Willson less than a month after his arrival, 'but I enjoy hockey here ten times more than I did in your kingdom'. It was not only that the Schweriners thought him the best outside-right for ten miles round, but also that they played hockey in an entirely different spirit from Marlborough: 'Yes, hockey means a different thing than that cold-blooded performance on winter evenings beneath the eyes of an Officious and Offensive House-Captain, that it used to mean. We now play twice a week, beginning at three

[1] Forbidden.

112

o'clock and continuing until the sun goes down'. Sorley's
only complaint was about the clothes he had to wear:

> I was stealing out of the house [he told Hutchinson]
> looking very nice in clean white shorts (with a patch)
> and my cap-jersy[1] —looking quite Byronic. No sooner
> had I closed the door, than I was ruthlessly hauled
> back by the Frau's brother with averted eyes lest he
> might see my nakedness, and told that in Deutsch-
> land knees were not exhibited and ordered to change
> into breeches at once.

This formality became a source of amusement to Sorley
and symbolic of the difference between the races:

> The three German officers that belong to the club
> play in their Sunday clothes—boiled shirts, butterflies
> and spats. They have not yet hit the ball, but are still
> trying. Now isn't that delightful? Catch a beastly
> English officer making a public donkey of himself! I
> think it is the utter absence of self-consciousness that
> makes the Germans so much nicer than the English.

It was not only the hockey-players who delighted Sorley
in Schwerin. The shopkeepers also charmed him; he could
not buy a penny pencil without having to tell his life
history and hearing theirs in return. He thought the un-
affected way in which they laughed at him was probably
good for him, after the adulation he had had at Marlborough. One man asked him to come again 'because he
found it so funny hearing an Engländer trying to speak
Dutch', and thought he was complimenting him. 'The
common people are worth gold,' Sorley told Hutchinson.
'Only just now I "stepped" into a shop to "purchase"
this note-paper and had a splendid time with the shop-
keeper'. Not realizing that Sorley was a foreigner and

---

[1] A cap-jersy was worn by the possessors of a 'forty-cap' or 'sixty-
cap', which were the equivalent of the second fifteen or third
fifteen, respectively, at rugby.

thinking him deaf, the shop-keeper had shouted at him for half-an-hour, eventually asking, was he a Swede?

> I thought the best way to still the tumult was to say, 'O yes, I'm a Swede'; so I said so. Then the tumult commenced anew only far louder and more unintelligible, for he was now filled with the idea that I must be very deaf. A horrible fear came over me that his wife might be Swedish and he had started talking Swedish to me, and I would be publicly exposed as a liar. But such fortunately was not the case; he was merely saying—I at last discovered—that probably I had a great many very nice Swedish friends. But my nerves were by now strained to breaking, so I hurriedly left the shop with my notepaper, murmuring indiscriminate praise in broken German of my very many Swedish friends. I am much intrigued by my Swedish friends, and am thinking of writing a book about them.

Joking apart, Sorley genuinely admired the kindness and simple goodness of the people. He particularly liked the unpretentiousness of the Schweriners and their refusal to accept pretentiousness in others. On one occasion, tired of being continually cross-examined about his likes and dislikes in food, he had told the Beutins 'that all food was alike' to him. When dared to repeat this blasphemy, he did so and left the room feeling rather pleased with himself. He remained a victor till the evening meal, when he found on his plate a huge loaf of bread and a mountain of butter: 'Nice things were offered round the table (particularly nice they were that evening),' he wrote home, 'but Ida was told not to offer them to me, for all food was alike to Mr Sorley. But I quickly recanted and grovelled, sold my soul for German sausage and climbed down'. It was useless trying to show off in the face of such directness and a relief to be honest about his love of food, as the Beutins were.

German soldiers impressed Sorley in a quite different

way, making him feel 'more unpatriotic daily'. Returning from a walk with Frau Beutin, he heard several
companies of soldiers singing: 'Were they singing?' he
asked Wynne Willson rhetorically. 'They were roaring—
something glorious and senseless about the Fatherland
(in England it would have been contemptible Jingo: it
wasn't in Deutschland), and all the way home we heard
the roar, and when they neared the town the echo was
tremendous. Two hundred lungs all bellowing. And when
I got home, I felt I was a German, and proud to be a
German: when the tempest of the singing was at its
loudest, I felt that perhaps I could die for Deutschland—
and I have never had an inkling of that feeling about
England, and never shall'. As a Scot Sorley had never
identified with England, nor even with Scotland, which
he had left at the age of five. This was the first time he
had had 'the vaguest idea what patriotism meant—and
that in a strange land'.

Rather to his surprise Sorley enjoyed the German
language as much, if not more, than the people. He
began to think Atkey had been right in advising him to
stay at Marlborough, for he had neglected classics completely since his arrival in Schwerin. 'I am so intoxicated
by the beauties of the German language and by *John
Gabriel Borkman*' he admitted to Atkey, 'that I have
done nothing and thought nothing of Latin or Greek
since I came here: only Goethe and Heine and innumerable books about *John Gabriel Borkman*, and the play
itself, of course. But I hope to reform some time next
week. But at present this new language is quite enough
to keep me happy. Ibsen is a quite different thing altogether in German!' To begin with Frau Beutin had
concentrated on grammar in her lessons, though she also
read with Sorley a translation of *A Christmas Carol*,
which moved her, but not him, to tears! By himself he
read 'sterner stuff'—Goethe's *Egmont*, recommended and
lent to him by the Frau's brother. Whenever he had an

odd quarter of an hour he indulged himself in Heine's shorter lyrics. After a week of rapid progress he reports that 'the Frau and I read together silly novels in the morning in our Stunde, which generally stretches to three hours instead of one and a half: because she has an English translation with her. In the evening we read together lovely sentimental little things, easy to understand, from Heine and Geibel: and then I retire to my room at 9.30 (with the pleasant lie that I go to bed then) and hack my way through another scene from *Egmont*, which bears about as much resemblance to Geibel's lyrics as the downs to the forest at Marlborough: and then I generally (as now) write, when I ought to be in bed'.

Sorley's relations with the Frau were becoming daily more intimate. Though his initial impression of her 'braininess' had changed somewhat, his admiration for her character increased on further acquaintance: 'she is an extraordinarily nice woman and has a very pleasant face and figure,' he tells his parents a week after his arrival. Five days later he writes: 'The Frau Doktor and I are getting very thick. She is really an awfully nice woman, and very frank, and tells me whiles that I'm getting very "eingebildet"[1] . . . and asked me suddenly the other evening if my brother and sister always thought they were in the right as well'. While Herr Doktor Beutin is at the office from ten till four, Sorley has his lessons with the Frau, goes shopping with her, plays ridiculous games with names like 'Puffspiel' with her, then reads with her again in the evening—'lovely sentimental little things'. She begins to confide in him and to make him feel that he is necessary to her well-being:

Up to the time of my predecessor [he writes to his parents], the Frau had such a lonely life that I wonder she did not go mad or commit some fearful crime.

[1]Eingebildet: conceited.

Du lieber Karl is absent practically all day and so she was left with the red-armed many-fountained Ida (the general) for company. The Philolog works practically all day, and takes his Mittagsessen with his mama. So altogether an English companion is by now more or less a necessity to her, for her friends in Schwerin are Alexander Bells,[1] and she's not the kind of fat German Frau who's content with a life of husband-coddling and housework.

A month after his arrival Sorley's opinion has risen even higher. Any criticism he had of her intellect is quite forgotten. The Frau in her turn asks for a photograph of Sorley, which his mother sends, and then has numerous photographs of him taken herself, which she sends as a birthday present to Mrs Sorley. Frau Beutin also writes to Mrs Sorley, telling her how much she will miss 'Charlie' when he leaves: 'I always forget his age, he is in his spirit so much older and so we speak as if there were no difference in the age, you can be proud for him, his intellect, his heart and his behaviour'. In another letter she thanks Mrs Sorley for sending her her son—'the time with him was like a holiday and a feastday'.

Sorley's parents were slightly disturbed by the tone of these letters from Frau Beutin and their son, but sensibly they did not show it. There is no doubt that a close emotional attachment had grown up between the handsome young man of eighteen and the lonely middle-aged housewife, who had become rather overwrought in her isolation and her lack of outlet for her artistic yearnings. Sorley was by nature sympathetic, especially towards those who were unfulfilled. He was also grateful to the Frau for introducing him to the 'glorious' German lan-

---

[1]His name is Alexander Bell,
   His home, Dundee;
I do not know him quite so well
   As he knows me. (R.F. Murray, *The Scarlet Gown*)

guage in which they had read so much romantic literature together. Away from all his friends and family he turned to her for friendship. Yet it is highly unlikely that either of them were conscious of how far their relationship had developed though Sorley afterwards recognised in her 'an unsatisfied maternal instinct'. So mature in many ways, Sorley was almost completely inexperienced when it came to women. Apart from a few formal occasions, such as 'coming-out' dances at Cambridge, he had had very little contact with them. There was nothing unusual in this at a time when relations between the sexes generally started much later, especially among the middle classes. Frau Beutin, too, appears to have been an innocent. She and the Herr Doktor had been engaged 'like Jacob and Rachel for seven years,' Sorley told his parents, and had written to each other every day during that time. They had been married eight years when Sorley first met the Frau. She never criticised her husband to Sorley, but it is clear that he did not satisfy her deeper needs.

Sorley himself became highly critical of the Herr Doktor after his initial enthusiasm. So critical in fact that one cannot help suspecting that, consciously or unconsciously, he was jealous of him. He found Frau Beutin's admiration of her husband 'quite pathetic' and his second sketch of the Doktor to his parents is heavily ironic:

The Herr Doktor is one of the men who, I imagine, make Germany what She Is. He gets up at 8.30, and goes to his office before 10. There he works till half-past-three or often till half-past four, and then returns for Mittagsessen, in a state of overwhelming perspiration due, his wife tells me, to overwork. He works again from five till half-past seven, and after Abendessen, followed by a brief but memorable innings at the harmonium, goes into his room and works till

2 a.m. All this, as far as I can make out, is the dullest kind of work—chiefly copying and correspondence and dull little provincial law-suits about step-mothers, which get explained at Abendessen. He is very genial—I think 'genial' is the right word—and behaves to his wife exactly like Torvald Helmer[1] calling her 'sweet mouse' and 'comic child'. However she is fortunately no Norah—and is 'thankful oh! so thankful' (she has told me) that her man is always happy and hearty, and not as other women's husbands are, who come back violent (as well as sweaty) from their day's work.

From being 'perfectly delightful' the Doktor becomes 'stupid', an 'old fool . . . whose mind has failed to expand since the age of six' and Sorley's respect for the Frau 'does not embrace her worser half'. He particularly objects to the Doktor's morning endearments:

He comes down to Frühstück[2] late and looking enormously fat and vulgar, shouts out 'Liebling' at the top of his voice as soon as he catches sight of her, sweats with the effort, sits down heavily, and grasping a knife with clenched fist proceeds to state that he feels as 'fresh as dew!' (I have looked up the word and, with a different gender, it can also mean rope: take which you please.)

Sorley cannot bear the thought of Frau Beutin being mauled by the fat and sweaty Doktor, nor can he understand how such a fine spirit should be wasted on such a gross one. The Doktor now seems to him utterly absurd and he is continually poking fun at him—'hero' Karl goose-stepping in the reserves, 'dear' Karl receiving a medal for Faithfulness, 'schoolboy' Karl playing practical jokes and, best of all, 'greedy' Karl unable to resist cake:

[1] Ibsen's male chauvinist in *A Doll's House*.
[2] Frühstück: breakfast.

Last week-end was enlivened by a visit from Karl's little brother Hermann, who weighs 16 stone. . . . He was accompanied on arrival by a huge cake, not quite as big as himself, which he presented to the Frau, amid shrieks of delight from Karl, as a kind of entrance fee. It was a goo-ood cake, though I regret to say there were 'quarrels' over when it should be eaten—as a kind of pick-me-up between meals? or during Mittagsessen? and, if the latter, after the soup or with the coffee at the end? The latter was decided upon, till suddenly, half-way through Mittagsessen, Du Lieber Karl struck and insisted on having his piece before the oranges. Having had it, he repented and had another piece with us with the coffee. Clever man. The great question for discussion while Hermann was there was, which do you think is fatter, Karl or Hermann? They were eventually measured, and Hermann won. They are dears—but I prefer the Frau's side of the family.

It is clear from this last extract that Sorley did not actually dislike Karl; he merely despised him. In reading the *Odyssey* he is reminded of Karl by 'poor pompous Menelaus'. Frau Beutin is, of course, Helen of Troy and Sorley himself probably Hector: 'I'm sure she was always dull down in Sparta with fatherly old Menelaus,' he theorises, 'though she never showed it, of course. But there is always something a little wistful in her way of speaking. She only made other people happy and consequently another set of people miserable. One of the best things in the *Iliad* is the way you are made to feel (without any statement) that Helen fell really in love with Hector—and this shows her good taste, for of all the Homeric heroes Hector is the only unselfish man'. Sorley says specifically in another letter home that the Beutins remind him of characters from the *Odyssey*. In fact the whole tone of the book he finds 'thoroughly

German and domestic'. In both there is the same hospitality, love of eating, telling long stories and giving of gifts: 'so I am really reading it in sympathetic surroundings,' he tells Wynne Wilson, 'and when I have just past the part where Helen shows off to Menelaus her new work-basket that runs on wheels, and the Frau rushes in to show me her new water-can with a spout designed to resemble a pig—I see the two are made from the same stuff (I mean, of course, Helen and Frau B., not Frau B. and the pig)'.

Sorley's first strong attraction towards a woman did not, as far as we know, prompt him to write passionate love poetry. Yet it is likely that the one poem he wrote in Schwerin was sparked off by his feeling for the Frau, since it reflects a certain passion lacking in his earlier work. 'Marlborough', as he called it, seems to have sprung from a deeper level of consciousness than his previous poems, particularly in its second section, as we shall see. This last poem of the early period is Sorley's most perfect expression of his feelings for the downs, perhaps because it followed a period of separation from them. In it he at last manages to convey his mystical sense of oneness with nature in a form which illuminates rather than obscures his vision. The secret is simplicity, a simplicity similar to that found in another visionary— Wordsworth who undoubtedly influenced Sorley in writing it. For in spite of the archaisms which continue to creep in, the language is direct, almost bald, and the message is clear without being banal:

> I, who have walked along her downs in dreams,
>   And known her tenderness, and felt her might,
> And sometimes by her meadows and her streams
>   Have drunk deep-storied secrets of delight,
>
> Have had my moments there, when I have been
>   Unwittingly aware of something more,

Some beautiful aspect, that I had seen
   With mute, unspeculative eyes before;

Have had my times, when, though the earth did wear
   Her self-same trees and grasses, I could see
The revelation that is always there,
   But somehow is not always clear to me.

Sorley expresses his sense of revelation and rescues the
poem from monotony in the second section by introducing the story of Jacob, who wrestles in the night with a
stranger and in the morning has grown:

   A more immortal vaster spirit, who
      Had seen God face to face, and still lived on.

As Professor J.A. Stewart wrote to Geoffrey Bickersteth,
the story of Jacob 'is a sudden Trance-image, rising up
out of the depth . . . springing spontaneously out of his
emotion'. In the third and final section, which is only
half the length of the first two, Sorley shows us the
effect of his vision. He has at last resolved the conflict
he felt between the world of poetry and that of action,
for he now realises that it is his *duty* to write, that writing
is in a sense acting to the best of his ability:

   So, there, when sunset made the downs look new
      And earth gave up her colours to the sky,
   And far away the little city grew
      Half into sight, new-visioned was my eye.

   I, who have lived, and trod her lovely earth,
      Raced with her winds and listened to her birds,
   Have cared but little for their worldly worth
      Nor sought to put my passion into words.

   But now it's different; and I have no rest
      Because my hand must search, dissect and spell
   The beauty that is better not expressed,
      The thing that all can feel, but none can tell.

Sorley spent far more time reading than writing, however, in Schwerin. He had started to read the *Odyssey*, for instance, mainly out of shame. His fellow hockey-players had asked him to repeat the first line of the text 'that they [might] mark the difference between the German and English pronunciation of Greek'—which he could not do. When he saw how they pitied him for his lack of learning, even though he was the best outside right for miles around, he appreciated the irony: 'at Marlborough I was if anything on the side of the angels who knew the first line of the *Odyssey*, and now I am among those whose hockey is their fortune'. In spite of his unwillingness to take up classics again, he was provoked into buying a threepenny Homer, which he began to read. For the first time since he started studying classics he really enjoyed it: 'The *Odyssey* is a great joy when once you can read it in big chunks,' he wrote home, 'and not a hundred lines at a time, being able to note all the silly grammatical strangenesses or else a pained Master'. He also read Euripides and Aeschylus, but in spite of a curt letter from his future tutor at Oxford, he found it very difficult to take up Latin again. Demosthenes and Cicero could wait until autumn.

Sorley was far more interested in German literature. He found the Frau's brother more helpful in this respect than the Frau. She tended to concentrate on lyric poetry and 'silly novels', whereas the Neuphilolog introduced Sorley to Goethe, first reading to him, then lending him *Egmont*. Sorley also read *Faust* with the Frau, but the Neuphilolog kept a close eye on them: 'He examines me and the Frau every evening on what we have read and our understanding thereof,' he told his family, 'and turns a deaf ear to his sister's chaff. I never knew how nice and natural and interesting a pedant could be till I met the Philolog'. To begin with Sorley found *Faust* 'more a wonderful collection of "very good remarks" than a dramatic masterpiece', but as he read on he realised its greatness: 'There is nothing I have ever thought or ever read that is not somewhere contained in it, and (what is worse) explained in it'. In the light of *Faust* his own efforts at poetry seemed insignificant and he was discouraged from further attempts for the time being: 'The worst of a piece like *Faust* is that it completely dries up any creative instincts or attempts in oneself'.

Sorley had not really begun to understand *Faust* until he saw it performed in Schwerin. The local theatre, which was subsidised by the Grand Duke, was very enterprising for a small town. It was open five nights a week from October to May and put on serious plays. Sorley felt he would never forget his first visit on 13 February 1914: '. . . all other dramatic performances have been shoved into the shade for me since yesterday,' he told Atkey, 'when I went to *John Gabriel Borkman* at the theatre here . . .' Having read the play in German, which he thought far superior to the English translation, he could follow well and wrote enthusiastically:

> I think it is far finer than any other of Ibsen's. And it has far more poetry in it than the others I have read, even though there is the inevitable bank-smash in the background. The acting couldn't have been better— and the phlegmatic and un-emotional way those Teutons received the piece! I dared to clap, not Philistinely in the middle of a scene, but decently at the end of the play, and all the eyes of the theatre were turned upon me.

He found the technique of the play perfect—'it bristles with minor problems'. And he shows the same technical interest in all the other plays he sees at Schwerin, ranging from Shakespeare's *Richard III* to Hebbel's *Gyges und Sein Ring* and Schiller's *Wilhelm Tell*. He had been interested in drama at Marlborough, where he had helped reform the dramatic society. (The Master had stipulated this must be called the Shakespeare Society, as he con-

sidered the word 'dramatic' was 'disturbing'.) The society
had not managed to put on any performances in Sorley's
time, but they had read plays together—*Richard III* and
The Enemy of the People among others. Sorley had also
read Synge, whom he enjoyed. However he found Masefield a much stronger playwright and equally poetical.
Masefield's *Tragedy of Nan* was 'a marvellous play to
read' and would, he believed, be 'even better on the
stage'. Masefield was almost certainly a model for Sorley's
own experiment in verse drama at Marlborough—*The
Other Wise Man*. Its religious content, its lack of division
into scenes, its somewhat vague setting and use of blank
verse all suggest that Lascelles Abercrombie was another
influence. Sorley had just finished reading and admiring
Abercrombie's 'The Tale of Saint Thomas' in *Georgian
Poetry 1* when he began his own verse drama. 'The
Other Wise Man' lacks dramatic tension but is an excuse
for some lovely passages of blank verse and an exposition
of Sorley's religious views[1] :

THE OTHER WISE MAN

A vale of tears, they said!
A valley made of woes and fears,
To be passed by with muffled head
Quickly. I have not seen the tears,
Unless they take the rain for tears,
And certainly the place is wet.
Rain-laden leaves are ever licking
Your cheeks and hands . . . I can't get on.
There's a toad-stool that wants picking.
There, just there, a little up,
What strange things to look upon
With pink hood and orange cup!
And there are acorns, yellow—green . . .
They said the King was at the end.
They must have been

[1] See page 85.

Wrong. For here, here, I intend
To search for him, for surely here
Are all the wares of the old year,
And all the beauty and bright prize,
And all God's colours meetly showed,
Green for the grass, blue for the skies,
Red for the rain upon the road;
And anything you like for trees,
But chiefly yellow, brown and gold,
Because the year is growing old
And loves to paint her children these.

Sorley did not continue his experiments in drama but he retained a strong interest in it, which was more than satisfied at Schwerin. He devoted a great deal of his time there to reading and analysing plays in German, so that he could appreciate them fully when performed.

Sorley's German and Greek studies left him very little time for English literature. This was deliberate, as he told Atkey:

I am only reading English on Sundays when all Germany is asleep after Mittagsessen. I think it is then permissible. In the holidays, I shunted Masefield into a siding and 'discovered' Hardy. Since then, like people in the advertisements, I have read no other.

Writing to another friend about the 'model Christian life' he is leading in Schwerin Sorley concludes: 'However, I cannot do without a little touch of heathenism, and so (although I swore to read no English here) I do just occasionally give myself up to Thomas Hardy and am falling more and more under his influence'. It was Hardy's response to the Pagan remains and primitive customs of the west country, parts of which border on Marlborough, and his refusal to accept a comforting interpretation of life that attracted Sorley, who began to identify closely. 'T.H. has temporarily taken possession of myself,' he told

1. and 2. Charles Sorley's parents, Professor and Mrs W.R. Sorley, *c.* 1913

3. Mrs Sorley with, left to right, Jean, Kenneth and Charles
4. Left to right: Kenneth, Jean and Charles Sorley; the twins are
about 2½ to 3½ years old. Taken in Aberdeen

5. Group taken on the steps of Powis House, Old Aberdeen, 1898, *l. to r.*:
Ellen Cheyne (cook), Lizzie Porter (Nanny Porters's sister and under-nurse),
Charles Sorley, Maddy Melville (housemaid), Jean and Kenneth Sorley and
Nanny Jean Porter.
6. The Greek Manse, Old Aberdeen, 1899, *l. to r.*: Jean, Kenneth and
Charles

7. Glenbulig, Ballater, 1899
l. to r.: Kenneth, Jean and
Charles Sorley and their
Dunlop Smith cousins,
Norah and Janet
8. Nanny Porter with
Dorothy and Jackie Butler,
July 1919

9 (top). *L. to r.*: Jean, Kenneth, Charles, Prof. and Mrs Sorley, playing croquet on their lawn at St Giles, Cambridge, 1903
10 (left). Cricket at Dunwich, 1906. Charles and his cousin, John Meredith Townsend (batting) 11 (right). Charles at Dunwich, 1906

12. Kenneth and Charles at Dunwich, 1906

13. Kenneth and
Charles at Dunwich,
1906

14. The Greek Manse, 1908, *l. to r.*: Prof. Sorley, Charles and Kenneth
15. The Greek Manse, 1908, *l. to r.*: Kenneth, Charles, Grey Pussy, Jean and Prof. Sorley

16. The Greek Manse, 1908, *l. to r.*: Kenneth, Charles, Grey Pussy, Dildar and Jean
17. Cambridge, 1908, *l. to r.*: Mrs Sorley, Charles, Jean, Kenneth and Prof Sorley

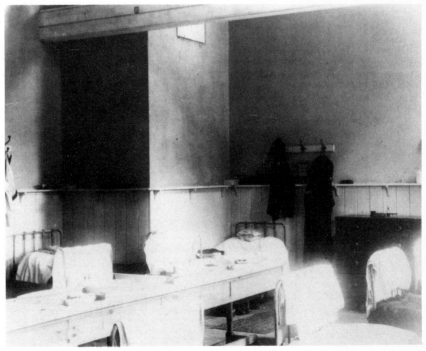

18. Marlborough High Street, *c.* 1915
19. A typical dormitory at Marlborough College, *c.* 1915. Note the O.T.C. uniform hanging in the corner

20. Charles (top left) and Mr A.R. Gidney (top right), detail from C1
House Football photograph, 1912
21. O.T.C. Camp at Churn, Berkshire, 1913: Charles third from left,
barefooted

22. Front of C House, Marlborough College, taken from the Central Avenue
in Court, *c.* 1915

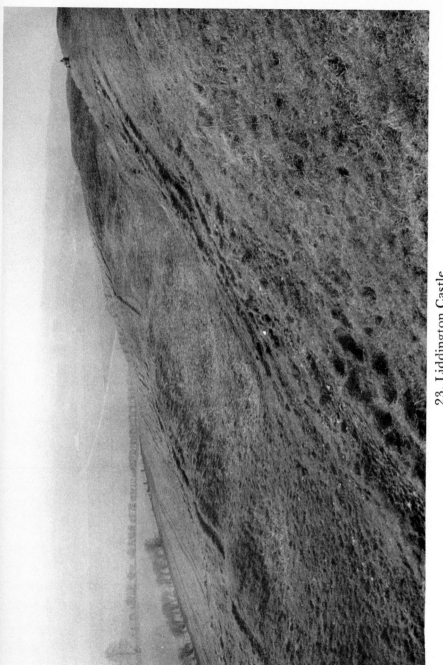

23. Liddington Castle

Marlborough

§ 1

Crouched where this open upland billows down
Into the valley where the river flows,
She is as any other country town,
That little lives or marks or hears or knows.

And she can teach but little. She has not
The wonder and the surging and the roar
Of striving cities. Only things forgot
That once were beautiful, but now no more,

Has she to give us. Yet to one or two
She first brought knowledge, and it was for her
To open first our eyes, until we knew
How great, immeasurably great, we were.

I, who have walked along her downs in dreams
And known her tenderness, and felt her might,
And sometimes by her meadows and her streams
Have drunk deep-storied secrets of delight:

Have had my moments there, when I have been
Unwittingly aware of something more,
Some beautiful aspect, that I had seen
With mute unspeculative eyes before;

Have had my times, when, though the earth did wear
Her self-same trees and grasses, I could see
The revelation that is always there,
But somehow is not always clear to me.

§ 2

So, long ago, one halted on his way
And sent his company and cattle on;
His caravans trooped dwindling far away
Into the night, and he was left alone.

24. Opening page of MS. of 'Marlborough'

25. East Kennet church at evening
26. Detail from C House photograph, *c.* 1912; Charles seated centre bottom row

27 (top left). Charles Sorley, Folkestone, 1914
28 (top right). Charles at Schwerin, Easter 1912
29. Charles, Autumn 1914

30. Charles, Autumn 1914

Hutchinson on 26 February 1914: 'horrid old pessimist and scoffer though he is, there is no one like him—except yours ever'. To begin with he preferred the earlier novels, particularly *Far From the Madding Crowd*, but after a second reading of *Jude the Obscure* he decided that it was 'quite the finest novel' and on a level with *Oedipus*, *Lear* and *Othello*: 'The glory of the book is its failure: I mean that Hardy, setting out to show that it were better for Jude if he had never been born, shows exactly the reverse'. Sorley's detailed criticism of the book and his annotations show the same technical interest in the novel as he had shown in the drama. And, if we are to take his letter of 7 February to Hutchinson seriously, he had already written three chapters of a novel himself. His views on the novel are clear-cut; he knows why he prefers Hardy to Dickens and Meredith, for example—because he does not, as they do, 'inject his own exaggerated characteristics' into his characters. In his enthusiasm for Hardy Sorley tried to make converts, as he had with Masefield: when he heard that Kenneth had to go into a nursing home he begged his parents: 'Do force him to take some Hardy . . . I'm sure that with *Far From the Madding Crowd* and *The Trumpet Major* . . . Nursing Home were paradise enow'. After four months' close study of Hardy, however, that 'horrid old pessimist and scoffer' went the way of Masefield. Goethe next became Sorley's 'favourite prophet' and remained so for the rest of his life.

Hardy was not the only instance of Sorley's volatile tastes and opinions at this time. After two months of unqualified praise for the Schweriners—with the exception of the Herr Doktor—Sorley begins to realize their limitations, which had seemed at first meeting quaint idiosyncrasies. And curiously enough he lays part of the blame on his hero, Goethe:

This provincial part of Germany [he writes to Atkey]

does not seem to me to have yet recovered from the influence of Goethe and Schiller. Their family guide to conduct is the *Lied von der Glocke*, which has such a horribly domestic conventional and compromising tone, that I cannot stand it. Their outlook on life here seems to me 140 years old.

Sorley was in particular weary of the Beutins.' 'gay' Lent parties, for obvious reasons:

The German supper is a terror [he tells Hutchinson]. The people come at seven and talk about the rise in the price of butter till 8. From 8 till 9.30 they eat and drink and talk about the niceness of the victuals, and ask the hostess their cost. From 9.30 to 10.30 they talk about the scarcity of eggs. From 10.30 to 11 they drink beer and cross-examine ME about the Anglo-German crisis. From 11 to 12 they make personal remarks and play practical jokes on one another. From 12 to 12.30 they eat oranges and chocolates and declare they must be going now. From 12.30 to 1 they get heavy again and sigh over the increased cost of living in Schwerin. At 1 they begin to scatter. By 2 I am in bed.

It seems to Sorley that among the upper classes of Schwerin the only person of any ideas is Frau Beutin. His use of the qualification 'among the Upper Classes' shows that he is beginning to realize the existence of a very different kind of person. 'Down in the "slums" of Schwerin they seem to be a very breezy lot,' he tells Atkey. 'They have religious debates every week, which I am now allowed to attend, and distinguished agnoggers from the south come and speak to them.' It had been at the first of these debates, led by an agnostic called Professor Drews, that Sorley had first suspected the existence of another side of Schwerin:

It is not such a provincial place as I thought by any means. It seems that it is only the lawyers and officers—

the highest grade socially—that are the lowest intellectually. Those people in the Vortag[1] . . . with whom we don't 'sociate—actors, journalists, Jews—seem to lead a much freer life than their social superiors. I got a little scolded by the Herr Doktor for clapping Otto Drews; he was much disgusted by the whole thing, and *schimpfed* dreadfully. But it was nice of him to come, for he didn't want to.

Sorley was to admit towards the end of April that his 'previous enthusiasm has been sobered to a decent critical appreciation of German provincial life, which is still delightful from a spectator's point of view—but preserve me from having to live it for ever!' Nevertheless, he was fond of what he called 'my people' and extended his visit as long as he could. He enjoyed Easter with the Beutins, not because he liked searching for stale marzipan eggs, but because of the visit of the Doktor's old student friend—the 'admirable Klett', who arrived as the Easter hare. 'The way this extraordinarily alert and bustling man from Berlin laughed down all Karl's Mecklenburgish ideas was charming to see,' he told his parents. 'Karl is only gradually recovering. He was a really perfect guest and most interesting man.'

At the end of April Sorley welcomed Kenneth, who was to replace him at Schwerin and thus console the Frau. Charles then left for Jena, where he was to spend another three months studying at the university. Having encountered so many new experiences and absorbed so much in Schwerin, the time had passed very quickly for him there. Apart from his attempt to express what Marlborough meant to him, in the poem of that name, he had produced no new work. There are a few facetious verses to friends, it is true, but most of his writing consists of letters, which are sparkling and witty records of a way of life that was soon to be swept away. Sorley blamed

[1] Vortag: lecture.

Goethe's greatness for what he regarded as a 'drying-up' of his creative instincts, but it is a misrepresentation of the case. His creative instincts had not dried up; they had been channeled in a different direction. For this was Sorley's first encounter with the outside world and he needed all his energy to meet it, as he did, with enthusiasm and openness. When he starts to write poetry again it is not as a precocious schoolboy but as a young man enriched by a wide variety of new experiences.

7
Jena

When Sorley arrived in Jena at the end of April 1914, he was aware of an Anglo-German crisis: he did not anticipate a cataclysm. Relations between the two countries had been deteriorating, but not even the statesmen could have predicted that the assassination of an Austrian Archduke by a Serbian patriot would precipitate England into a full-scale war.

Sorley was more concerned about the problems of settling in at Jena. To begin with he had not welcomed his parents' decision to send him there: 'Is Jena more or less settled as my fate?' he asks them in February 1914. 'It is such a little quiet place, it seems. Fired by ecstatic accounts and post-card albums of the lemon-faced Philolog, my eyes turn longingly in the direction of Munich, which I have been led to understand is for some or another reason under a ban. And you don't have to walk thirteen miles to see a theatre.' When he hears that they speak 'an utterly alien language' in Munich, he is less anxious to go there, but still hopes for the northern capital, Berlin. His parents have decided on Jena, however, the then German equivalent of Oxford or Cambridge, and Sorley, as usual, accepts their decision: 'He that maun to Jena will to Jena.' He consoles himself with the thought that, with Weimar only fifteen miles away, this quiet university town in the south should be full of 'all the ghosts of all the Goethes and all the shades of all the Schillers'. As it turns out he is pleased with Jena and relieved that he has not gone to Berlin—'dowdy, jolly, bourgeois Berlin'—but it rankles slightly that his parents have given him no explanation for their decision. Since his new-found independence at Schwerin he feels he ought to have more say in matters.

Once Sorley got to Jena he had an even greater degree

of independence. For he was no longer living in the protective circle of a family as he had done at Schwerin, but entirely on his own. The Beutins were shocked at the idea of him going to hunt for a room in Jena by himself, though he was excited by the prospect. They insisted that the Philolog's 'Jonathan' at Jena should find a 'bed-sit' for him at a reasonable price. 'Jonathan has found me a room, 25 marks a month, coffee included,' Sorley reports to his parents at the end of April. 'I call that cheap. It remains to be seen whether it is nasty also. Jonathan says the view is beautiful, it is three floors up, and the sole objection is that the only entrance into the room is through the landlord's dining-room—but this is made a positive pleasure by the wonderful charm of the landlord.' Rather to Sorley's surprise the 'land*lord*' turned out to be a lady and something of a puzzle. When he asked for her name she said Frau *Dr* Glänze, which fired Sorley's quick fancy: 'She certainly speaks decent German, but *Dr* is rather a mouthful. And where is the Herr Dr? Is she a widow? and if so, why does she dress in pink? Or does Herr Dr (perhaps a dentist!) live a double life? She has two children and an arm-chair containing a pale thin woman who only smiles. There is certainly an infinite field for research here'. Whatever her past the landlady proved kind, giving Sorley for his nineteenth birthday 'heaps of cakes, exuding sweetness, with which I don't quite know what to do'. In return Sorley perjured himself for her, swearing before forty German officials that her pet squirrel was not a nuisance, but had the 'manners of a lamb and smel[t] like eau de Cologne'. His grateful landlady presented him with a large bunch of sweet peas. The room itself was satisfactory, though rather small. 'I am now giving full play to my nasty Scotch (sorry, Scots) instincts,' he confesses to Hutchinson a few days after he has settled in:

I have a bed-sit., the size of that dejected bathroom

where the one new boy in house may be found washing at any hour of the day—which costs me with breakfast, 25 mks. a month. . . . The only objection to my bed-sit. is that it leads off a room which at different hours of the day plays the rôle of dining-room, sitting-room, nursery and bathroom—a most versatile room—let us call it 'parlour'. Whenever I pass through it, as I must pretty frequently, there are always five to eight children in it who spring to their feet and remain in an attitude of 'attention' till, murmuring words of praise, I at last escape. The only other way out of my room is a daring leap through the window on to the roof of an out-house. So now I see why the price of the room is so inordinately cheap.

Sorley's parents had brought him up to be careful though not mean with money and he is pleased to show how well he can manage it by himself. He discovers cheap places to eat—an inn for lunch, where the food is good and plentiful but badly served, and a café for his evening meal, where he can get poached eggs, potatoes, cutlets, soup, cocoa and other tasty things.

To begin with Sorley is delighted by Jena. The impression of mediaevalism which he got from the train on entering Thuringia was increased on examining the town. 'It lies somewhat like Ballater,' he tells his parents, 'and there are, or ought to be, castles on all the surrounding hills. The streets are narrow and gaily-coloured and almost roofed with flags. Then these absurd people with bright ribbons and caps and wounded faces[1] make it look eighteenth century'. This impression of mediaevalism is soon dispelled and he begins to find the town, which is in a hollow surrounded by hills, oppressive. It now seems to him like a saucer 'whose rim and centrepiece are mediaeval—all between is of the rankest suburban villa type'.

The people, however, he finds stimulating. They make

[1] Duelling was still practised by some German students.

him realize that the German 'isn't such a fool' as he had begun to think him after three months in Schwerin. His contact with Jena is mainly with university people, which probably accounts for his change of opinion. The first lecturer he listens to, Nohl, for instance, seems to him 'most attractive and alive'.

Sorley had gone to hear Nohl give the first of a course of lectures on Ethics in defiance of the University authorities. For when he presented himself at the appropriate office and showed them his Higher Certificate they refused to matriculate him or even to allow him to attend lectures until he got a passport.[1] In despair Sorley searched out an English lecturer Arthur Watts, whom he hoped might help him. After ploughing through muddy streets he eventually found Watts's house, but took an instant dislike to it. He pictured 'an elderly Englishman and fat, accustomed to Extension lecturing, sitting over weak tea and sponge-cakes with a German wife—and turned back'. In half an hour he returned, however, to find Watts quite different from his imaginings. Not only was he unmarried, but he was neither elderly nor fat. 'You were forty when I first saw you,' Sorley recalled later: 'thirty, donnish and well-mannered when you first asked me to tea: but later, at tennis, you were any age: you will be always forty to strangers perhaps: and you then as you get to know them'. In spite of appearing 'donnish' Watts had no university education. He was self-educated and proud of it, tending to look down his pince-nez at Oxford or Cambridge graduates, to Sorley's delight. Watts was in poor health when they first met and this together with other problems made life difficult for him, as Mrs Sorley noted: 'I hope he will overcome the dumb spirit and be able to express himself,' she wrote to Geoffrey Bickersteth, who got to know Watts later, 'your sympathies will help him to that. My husband says he has too much ego in his cosmos; but one cannot

[1] It was still possible to travel without a passport in June 1914.

wonder at that when one knows what his life and
experiences have been. To me the wonder is that he is
so little cynical, so alive to beauty and wisdom and so
really humorous'. Sorley found him all these things and
more. Watts seems to have both liberated and stimulated
him during his stay at Jena. He saw Watts as a pioneer,
to whom he looked up, as Odysseus's comrades looked
up to him. It was certainly an intense relationship and
one which Sorley felt it important to keep up long after
he left Jena. Some of his best letters from France are
written to Watts, to whom he seemed able to reveal his
deeper emotions. He longed to see Watts again with all
the intensity of a separated lover. Yet there was nothing
overtly homosexual about their relationship. It was rather
the response of an eager young man to a sympathetic,
intelligent and imaginative person.

When they first met in Jena Watts showed his sympathy
by helping Sorley with his matriculation problems. 'The
English lecturer was very kind,' Sorley reports home a
week later, and even went to the extent of concocting a
"pleasant lie" on my behalf to satisfy the abominable
clerk, who at last matriculated me'. He can now write
'From Herrn stud. phil. C.H. Sorley' to Hutchinson:
'Notice the above address and mind you put it all on the
envelope if, after seeing all my titles, you feel exalted
enough to write to me again. Isn't it delightful? I am
simply beaming at the thought of getting an envelope
addressed like that. And it only cost twenty marks. For
a mere twenty marks, I received a long list of injunctions,
among others that all correspondence to me should be
addressed thus'.

At Schwerin Sorley had begun to enjoy learning; at
Jena, ironically, he appears to be less keen. Marlborough
had bred in him a dislike of organised study, which
emerges again in this ancient university town. 'I attend
lectures on philosophy and political economy in the intervals of tennis and talking,' he writes rather defiantly to

Gidney: 'and may sometimes also be found reading in the *Odyssey* in my cheap little bed-sit. I have gladly forgotten all my Latin, and don't ever want to remember it again. I bear it a grudge. It's been the ruin of the English language. Just compare our compound words with the German ones! Ours are two dead dried Latin words soldered together. The German compound words are two or more living current German native words grafted one upon another and blooming together so that their separated and common sense can be grasped at the same time whenever one uses them. But I keep up my Homer, Aeschylus, and Euripides and wish I had brought some Plato with me. I read no English, though I miss our prose'. Sorley had been delighted to find the only suitable lecture on classical literature had been cancelled. 'The other men on the subject are quite impossible,' he excused himself to his parents, '—quarrelsome and dry and lecture over post-classical people'. He could not bear the way the German professors 'attacked' classics 'from a strictly antiquarian and textual and grammatical point of view', so in spite of a 'threatening' letter from his Oxford tutor, he decided to 'let classics take their chance'. Instead he concentrated on Philosophy, influenced no doubt by his father's love of it. Prof. Sorley had given him a letter of introduction to Prof. Rudolf Eucken, who ranked high as a philosopher in England. Sorley was disappointed in Eucken's Introduction to Philosophy course, which he found 'entirely amateurish', and his Metaphysics, which he could not follow. Eucken, he gradually realized, was the 'great joke' of Jena and 'the idea of calling him a philosopher laughed to scorn' he told Gidney, who worshipped Eucken as reverently as he did Pater and Ruskin:

And the same kind of fury that is aroused in me by their admiration of Byron as our greatest poet, is aroused in them by our opinion of Eucken as their

greatest living philosopher. Being an essential com-
promist, I suppose, he doesn't please the systematic,
downright, and uncompromising German nature. But
they tell us that, as England has no philosophy of its
own, they are quite pleased to give us one of their
comfortable half-prophet-half-philosophers to help our
amateurishness along!

Still Sorley thought Eucken 'a wonderfully beautiful
old man to look at, and comparatively mild' and he
eventually dared to present him with his father's letter.
Eucken promptly invited Sorley to his Sunday afternoon
'tea', a famous social occasion in Jena.

I dutifully went [he told his parents] and arriving on
the stroke of five was there first. Eucken was exception-
ally kind to me and spoke very nicely about you. But
soon floods of all peoples, nations, and languages
arrived—Greeks, Turks, Russians, Americans, and Japs
—and it developed into a most exciting crush. I picked
up several interesting students there who, apart from
a tendency to cross-examine, were very good company;
especially one who was looking for tennis and, with
the help of me and two others, has now found it. Mrs
Eucken is a Greek and rather like one of their statues
to look at. Miss Eucken, equally tall, and loosely,
almost dangerously, clad in an aggressive green dress
that went in hoops, sat beneath a tree, smoking loudly
and cracking brilliant epigrams with young privat-
dozents[1] while others hovered in the neighbourhood
and clapped. She smashed chairs, and shouted loudly
to her grey Greek mother on the other side of the
garden. But a very lively lady, and perhaps I do her
injustice with my similes, for she rode the whirlwind
and directed the storm quite well. Well, we all walked
about the garden and talked, and I answered a thousand
leading questions and arranged about tennis, and the

[1] Unsalaried university lecturers.

crowd did not diminish till a quarter to eight. So it was a most pleasant Sunday afternoon.

Sorley was amused to learn that 'all the freaks of Jena' were said to be found at Eucken's teas. He himself was most grateful for them, since he had made a few friends there and arranged to play tennis. Once games ceased to be compulsory and competitive, as they had been at Marlborough, he began to enjoy them. Now that hockey had ended he was anxious to find a substitute. So he and the student he had met at Eucken's arranged with Watts and his protégé to play tennis every morning from 7 to 8.45 a.m.—Sorley 'having crossed off a rather daundering set of lectures on Aesthetik to indulge in Athletik'.

Sorley also made friends at the several societies he had joined. His first attempt to become a member of the 'Freie Studentschaft'[1] was disastrous. To begin with he had walked into the wrong room—'where a mutual consolation meeting of future clergymen was going on'. When he eventually found the right room he made an even worse blunder, as he confessed to Hutchinson, though not to his parents:

> So I stumbled up to the door and met a waiter coming out. You know that I'm a crushed lily in the hands of waiters, tailors, etc. So when he asked me what I would have, I replied a glass of beer and stumbled into the hall. There sat thirty fat-faced youths, consuming lemonade. One of them was on his legs, and enjoying himself immensely talking. I found afterwards that the subject of his address was Youth and Temptation . . . And then my glass of beer came and cost me twopence-halfpenny. All eyes were turned towards the late-comer. The speaker stopped his discourse. What need had he to continue when Youth and Temptation were there incarnated before him? Dead silence. A copy of the rules was slowly passed down to Youth.

[1] Lit. Free Student Association.

Youth blushed heavily; in fact he almost cried, so naughty did he feel. The waiter was recalled and two-pence-halfpenny Temptation was removed. The Jenaer Freistudentenschaft breathed again. The speaker resumed his discourse, and the waiter re-appeared at Youth's elbow asking whether he preferred orangeade, grape-squash or onion-champagne. What a fool I was! Of course I should have known that all cheap clubs are temperance. However, after talking for three hours and a half, they brought off a pretty stroke of satire by drinking to the future of intellectual life in Jena in barley-water and lemonade.

Sorley cut all future meetings with what he called the 'fat sods' of the Freistudentenschaft. Instead he concentrated on another more exclusive club—the Freischar.[1] This consisted of about eight members, who lived and ate and worked together, and eight Extraordinary members, of which Sorley was privileged to become one. He had been introduced to the leader through Watts and was such a success at the first meeting that he was invited to attend weekly, rather than fortnightly as originally proposed. On their 'intellectual' evenings the members discussed Byron, Bulwer Lytton, Carlyle and 'other such discarded Englishmen who have found a home in Germany'. While not admiring any of these writers greatly, Sorley found the discussions stimulating and met one or two students whom he respected.

Sorley was quickly acquiring a large circle of acquaintances, but there was one type of student he avoided assiduously—'the "corps" student with beery wounded face'. He had been introduced to eight such on his first evening in Jena, when Jonathan and his friends had taken him for a 'joy-ride in a broken motor-car to a distant inn where they all went mad'. They drank a great deal 'but not enough to justify the amount of kissing that

[1] Lit. Free Group. Sorley elsewhere calls it 'a Carlyle Club'.

went on' Sorley felt '—kissing themselves and each other,
I mean, not their young women, which would have been
understandable'. His attitude to homosexuality, which he
must also have encountered in some form or other at
Marlborough indicates a lack of any tendency towards it
himself, in spite of his close attachment to Watts at this
time. When the corps students began to throw beer at
each other and exchange coats he began to see 'that one
must be kind to Germany, for it is very young and
getting on nicely with its lessons and so pleased with itself and just got into its private school cricket eleven'.
He was sure they were all 'good fellows' at heart. Nevertheless he did his best to avoid further contact with them
and when Wynne Willson attempted to defend them
Sorley retorts:

> You say that the 'corps' aren't bad really. But they
> are! Black-rotten! The sooner one dispels the libel on
> German universities that the corps student is the
> typical student, the better. They comprise only a third
> of the total number of students at Jena; and Jena is
> the most traditional of all German universities. They
> are the froth and the dregs. We, the 'nicht-inkorporier-
> ten', the other two-thirds, are the good body of the
> beer. We live in two feet square bedsits., we do a little
> work (impossible for the first three semesters for the
> corps students), and pretty soon we can mix with one
> another without any of the force and disadvantages
> of the artificially corporate life.

There may be an oblique reference to Marlborough College in this last sentence. Certainly Sorley goes on to say
that one of the things he most objects to is 'a peculiarly
offensive form of "fagging" for the six youngest students
in each corps', though he does not specify what this is.
The other aspect of the corps which revolts him is their
anti-semitism. For Sorley's friends at Jena are mostly
Jewish—'and so perhaps I see, from their accounts of the

insults they've to stand, the worst side of these many-coloured reeling creatures'. He sees in them the 'very worst result of 1871'[1] who show how 'Sedan has ruined one type of German', but consoles himself with the thought that they are dying out. 'One or two will still remain,' he predicts, 'for they're picturesque enough and their singing is fine: but please don't think they're typical of us'.

On the whole, however, he finds the students at Jena 'a most hospitable lot with extraordinarily alert and broad minds'. They have the same respect for learning that he had discovered in the Schwerin hockey-players, but they do not overwhelm him with patriotic talk or questions as the Schweriners had. His most exciting of 'one of a thousand discoveries' in Jena is that 'the superior better-blooded type of German Jew have far the finest minds of any people I have ever come across'. For in them he finds German thoroughness and love of learning combined with a humour and independence of mind he misses in the Germans themselves. Even Goethe, his favourite prophet, seems to him to lack the light touch: 'I am . . . sweatily struggling to the end of *Faust* II, where Goethe's just showing off his knowledge,' he tells his parents. 'I am also reading a very interesting book on Goethe and Schiller; very adoring it is, but it lets out quite unconsciously the terrible dryness of their entirely intellectual friendship and (Goethe's at least) entirely intellectual life. If Goethe really died saying "more light", it was very silly of him; what *he* wanted was more warmth'. Nevertheless Sorley continues to admire Goethe, particularly in *Faust*. The main idea of the play—'Er unbefriedigt jeden Augenblick'[2] —is entirely to his taste, for he still finds the idea of a restless and searching spirit

---

[1] 1871 was the date of the unification of Germany.
[2] He, every moment still unsatisfied.

as attractive as when he wrote 'Barbury Camp'.[1] Goethe also stimulates him to form 'a kind of amateur Weltanschauung'.[2] And it is here that he most admires the Germans, whatever their limitations: 'The average German does think for himself,' he tells Hutchinson. 'He doesn't simply live in the moment like the average Briton (which makes the average Briton pleasanter than the average German, but still!). And he does try to develop his own personality without reference to other people, that is, without making it either absolutely the same or absolutely different from his surroundings, as the Briton always does. They're really quite an admirable lot—and, when they try to be funny, they're like squeaking Teddy Bears'.

One of Sorley's first outings at Jena is a pilgrimage to Weimar, where Goethe had known Schiller and spent the last years of his life. Sorley's initial reaction to the place of pilgrimage is predictably perverse. He prefers the statue of Shakespeare to that of Goethe and Schiller embracing and spends far more time inspecting Prellers' wall-paintings of the *Odyssey* in the Weimar museum than he devotes to relics such as Schiller's discarded pyjamas. However he does take the trouble to inspect Goethe's house and he greatly enjoys seeing Goethe's *Iphigenie* performed at the Weimar theatre. He also enjoys other plays there later, in particular *The Merchant of Venice*. It is his continuing interest in drama which draws him back to Weimar whenever possible. 'I am so delighted by Weimar,' he tells Hutchinson after his second visit, 'that I imagine Zion is going to be a rather overdecorated Weimar. But in any case it can do no harm to anticipate the pleasure. And of course Weimar has the advantage over Zion of having a theatre and a very good one too'.

[1] See pages 102-3.
[2] Weltanschauung: world-view.

When Sorley visits Berlin at the beginning of June the theatre is one of the things he enjoys most, particularly Ibsen's *Peer Gynt*. His analysis of it shows his increasing discrimination:

> . . . the Northern Faust, as it is called: though the mixture of allegory and reality is not carried off so successfully as in the Southern Faust. Peer Gynt has the advantage of being a far more human and amiable creature, and not a cold fish like Faust. I suppose that difference is also to be found in the characters of the respective authors. I always wanted to know why Faust had no relations to make demands on him. *Peer Gynt* is a charmingly light piece, with an irresistible mixture of fantastical poetry and a very racy humour. The scene where Peer returns to his blind and dying mother and, like a practical fellow, instead of sentimentalizing, sits himself on the end of her bed, persuades her it is a chariot and rides her up to heaven, describing the scenes on the way, the surliness of St Peter at the gate, the appearance of God the Father, who 'put Peter quite in the shade' and decided to let mother Aasa in, was delightful. The acting was of course perfect.

Sorley had been invited to Berlin for Whitsuntide with Kenneth and the Beutins by Karl's friend the 'Admirable Klett'. The first night their host took them 'mercilessly from café to café . . . till early rosy-fingered dawn appeared'. After a second night's carousal Sorley 'struck' and went to bed. 'Having awoken refreshed at last,' he wrote to Wynne Willson, 'I found the rest of the party at last collapsed, huddled up in sofas and rocking-chairs, snoring, very happy. So now I am taking the opportunity of writing letters on my host's notepaper, while my host sleeps'. To begin with he had rather enjoyed the 'dowdiness' of Berlin. 'Those gay dogs that stay up all night are all so fat and bourgeois. Outside the army there seems none of that mixture of artificiality and vanity which we call smartness'. After four or five days of it he became more critical: 'There is nothing to see in Berlin,' he warned Hutchinson. 'It's a mistake to think it's the capital of Germany. It's the capital of Prussia and every Prussian is a bigot or a braggart—except the Prussian Jews: they alone have humour and independent minds. I like Germany too much to agree that Berlin is its capital. The town has no characteristics except efficiency and conceit and feeble imitation of French artistic vice, where the vice is doubled and the art dropped'. Once again we are reminded of his Calvinistic origins.

Back in Schwerin, where he was to spend a few days with Kenneth and the Beutins, he was surprised to find how much he liked it. There was something 'ursprunglich-ly[1] strong and poetical' in both the country and the people which Jena lacked, though its soil was 'rotten with the corpses of great men'. The Mecklenburg countryside was far more sympathetic to him than the Thuringian, which he found stiff and formal. 'I think Jena could only appeal to a Southern nature for long' he wrote home. 'When once one gets accustomed to its quaintness, there's nothing else left. And one is caught in a trap by all those seven (I suppose they are seven) hills that shut it round on every side, and I am far too lazy to climb them. When one does one only comes to woods with horrid stunted little trees, which are just like the top of the fashionable German's head with all the hair cut down'. Sorley was undoubtedly prejudiced in favour of Schwerin, partly by his devotion to Frau Beutin, partly by the 'tremendous reception' he received there from the hockey-players: 'all the fat old lawyers came and shook my paw and said they couldn't thank me enough for introducing the law of offside and sticks into Schwerin'. He was also delighted by his visit to a farm owned by a friend of the Beutins, where he was given one of the best meals of his

[1] Fundamentally.

144

life. When he recalled it afterwards it moved him almost
to poetry:

> [It was] in a farm-house utterly at peace in broad
> fields sloping to the sea. I remember a tureen of cham-
> pagne in the middle of the table, to which we helped
> ourselves with ladles! I remember my hunger after
> three hours' ride over the country: and the fishing-
> town of Wismar lying like an English town on the sea.
> In that great old farm-house where I dined at 3 p.m.
> as the May day began to cool, fruit of sea and of land
> joined hands together, fish fresh caught and ducks
> fresh killed: it was a wedding of the elements. It was
> perhaps the greatest meal I have had ever, for every-
> thing we ate had been alive that morning—the cham-
> pagne was alive yet. We feasted like kings till the sun
> sank, for it was impossible to overeat. 'Twas Homeric
> and its memory fills many hungry hours.

Once again we are reminded of the highly sensual side
of Sorley's nature, in strong contrast to his ascetic tend-
encies.

Despite his regret at leaving Schwerin in mid-June,
Sorley continued to appreciate Jena and his friends on
his return there. The weather had become oppressively
hot and thundery, proving an admirable excuse for in-
dulgence in his 'latest craze—German iced coffee with
whipped cream, all in a glass set before you in the ice-can
itself and drunk gently through a long tapering straw
(length three times that of a vulgar lemonade straw),
scented with mild tobacco'. Inspired perhaps by memories
of his Mecklenburg feast his thoughts turn to even greater
delicacies. 'It's only sheer lack of money that prevents
me feeding solely on iced coffee, mushrooms, peaches,
and champagne,' he tells Hutchinson. 'But having (through
a strange mixture of poverty and stinginess) to live on
boiled mutton, bad beer, poached eggs and divinely
virtuous soup, I have to make up by boring you by

accounts of the oysters and Rhine wine of my dreams'. As the heat builds up, he takes to eating supper at an inn on one of the surrounding hills, which adds to his expenses but cools him down. 'Otherwise life is one long perspiration which, I daresay, is very healthy,' he writes home. 'The Germans are all awfully happy hanging their hats on their tummies and promenading in the sun. But tennis continues, and I live *in* shorts and an unbuttoned shirt and *on* green salad and cherries'. The heat was occasionally relieved by a thunderstorm and in one of these moments of respite Sorley was moved to write a poem—the first attempt he had made to express his feelings about Germany in verse:

GERMAN RAIN

The heat came down and sapped away my powers.
The laden heat came down and drowsed my brain,
Till through the weight of overcoming hours
      I felt the rain.

Then suddenly I saw what more to see
I never thought: old things renewed, retrieved.
The rain that fell in England fell on me,
      And I believed.

Whilst retaining the simplicity which distinguished the Marlborough poems, this piece shows an increased technical skill, both in the choice of stanza with its unusually short fourth line and in its use of assonance. The oppressiveness of the heat is suggested by the regular, almost monotonous beat of the first verse, the repetition of long vowels and the repetition of the opening phrase in the second line. The coming of the invigorating rain is marked by the brief fourth line and the message of the poem is emphasised by placing it in the short last line of the second verse. Yet the effect remains clear and simple. The poem expresses Sorley's nostalgia for England, which is both increased and diminished by the rain. In reminding him of the Marlborough downs, where he found his own personal meaning in life, the rain helps him to invest life in Germany with the same significance. Yet he still longed 'to be sweating again on a rainy day in a minimum of garments from Barbury to Totterdown'.

'German Rain' was the first and last poem Sorley wrote in Jena. It may be that the heat 'drowsed [his] brain' to such an extent that he could not make the necessary effort. It is also likely that his busy social life left him very little time for solitary activities. Added to this was the discouraging effect of reading Goethe and other German poets. Sorley thought the Germans wrote better lyric poetry than the English, and spent most of his spare time in Jena reading it. He started with Rilke and Hölderlin, writing rather proudly to Gidney in June: 'I am getting down to the modern lyric writers now. There isn't a trick of the trade they don't know. I made a lengthy experiment one night when I was feeling silly: which resulted in the discovery that German has probably nearly twice as many rhyming words as we (at least beginning with the letter "a", which is as far as my experiment went). This gives them a horribly unfair advantage over us'. Sorley found their language 'colossally beautiful' and for a time he read nothing else. Like most of his enthusiasms, however, it passed quickly and by the beginning of July he was already critical of their technical skill, which he felt hid a lack of inspiration:

The language is massively beautiful, the thought is rich and sleek, [he wrote to Wynne Willson] the air that of the inside of a church. Magnificent artists they are, with no inspiration, who take religion up as a very responsive subject for art, and mould it in their hands like sticky putty. There are magnificent parts in it, but you can imagine what a relief it was to get back to Jefferies and Liddington Castle.

147

Satiated with German lyrics and scornful of their prose, which he found 'cobwebby stuff', Sorley had decided to indulge himself in one of his old favourites, Richard Jefferies. 'I want to read some good prose again,' he wrote to his parents. 'Also it is summer. And for a year or two I had always laid up "The Pageant of Summer" as a treat for a hot July. In spite of all former vows of celibacy in the way of English, now's the time. So, unless the cost of book-postage here is ruinous, could you send me a small volume of Essays by Richard Jefferies called *The Life of the Fields* . . . In the midst of my setting up and smashing of deities—Masefield, Hardy, Goethe—I always fall back on Richard Jefferies wandering about in the background'. When the book arrived, Sorley began to read it with his supper on the hill-top, and as he read his yearning for the Wiltshire downs grew stronger. The first essay in the collection, 'The Pageant of Summer', made him think of 'that part of the country where I should be now had Gidney had a stronger will than you,' he told his parents.

Sorley's other English favourite at this time was Shakespeare. As with Jefferies he had remained constant in his admiration of Shakespeare since Marlborough, but it was not until he saw him performed in Germany that he fully realized his greatness. *Richard III* at Schwerin had been followed by *The Merchant of Venice* at Weimar which, as Sorley's letter to Hutchinson shows, he understood for the first time:

. . . I had always thought before [it] was a most commonplace thing. Now I see it is far the biggest tragedy that Shakespeare ever wrote. The audience (especially a German audience) took part in the tragedy, because they laughed at Shylock and considered him a comic character throughout. As a glance at the life and methods of ordinary Christians it is simply superb. And the way the last act drivels out in a silly practical joke—while you know Shylock is lying in the same town deliberately robbed of all he cared for—is a lovely comment on the Christian life.

It was not until he saw *A Midsummer Night's Dream* that his enthusiasm reached its height. Professor and Mrs Sorley had visited him at the end of June and, quite by chance, had seen an open-air performance of the play announced in the local paper. 'It has put me off theatres for the rest of my life,' Sorley reported to Hutchinson afterwards. 'I laughed like a child and "me to live a hundred years, I should never be tired of praising it." The Germans are so Elizabethan themselves that their productions of Shakespeare are almost perfect. And in this case, the absence of curtains and scenery, and the presence of trees and skies, added the touch of perfection. Shakespeare's humour is primitive but, none the less, perfect'. To Wynne Wilson he was more specific:

After a great struggle, I have given the Germans Shakespeare! The deciding factor was the witnessing of *Midsummer Night's Dream* in a wood near Weimar. The Elizabethan spirit is not lost. It has only crossed the channel and found a home in Germany. Every Thuringian peasant is a Bottom or a Quince. I am never going into a theatre again, but shall always live on the recollection of that sublime and humorous benignity produced by the Thuringian Shakespeare, the Thuringian forest, and the Thuringian actors in concert. Shakespeare of the comedies *is* German. I am going to keep the histories, also *Lear* and the passionate tragedies, but give them *Hamlet* and the intellectual tragedies: and give them Shakespeare's humour, which does not depend (as the modern English) on malice and slyness. With Mendelssohn's music attached, it was the most harmonious thing I have ever seen.

When challenged by his parents on the superiority of

Goethe to Shakespeare, he evaded the question: 'I quite agree that *Faust* is far bigger than anything of Shakespeare's, but it was the work of sixty years, and *Hamlet*, I don't suppose more than six months'.

Shortly after Professor and Mrs Sorley left Jena for Berlin, Sorley received an unexpected letter from an old school friend, 'Hopper'. Arthur Hopkinson, who had arrived at Marlborough the same term as Sorley, had left the term before him. Though not in the same senior house, they had been together in the Sixth for two years and were evidently good friends. For Hopkinson had written to Sorley from Germany when he arrived there in August 1913. Since then he had led what Sorley jokingly called 'a varied life as cyclist, soldier, dramatic critic, criminal, and finally emigrant'. Having left for a short visit to England in June 1914, Hopkinson had returned to Germany for a three weeks' course at the University of Marburg and was writing to suggest a walking tour together at the end of July. 'Your Moselle plan has bucked me tremendously,' Sorley replied at once. 'Would it worry you very much to take a not *quite* final promise to partake? The reason is that I'm not really free for the first week in August, being booked for uninspiring visits. But I'm going to immediately (or immediately to) try and compass my emancipations. I think I'll easily get off, and then let you know for certain. I'm confident it will be yes! Then we can go into details'. The visits *were* cancelled, the details arranged and Sorley began to long for the end of term. He could at last confess, to his Aunt Minnie: 'I shan't be sorry to see an English penny again. There's something so honest and English and unpractical in a big downright English penny—so much nicer than those nasty little ten-pfennig pieces that are for ever making you think they're marks. A good breakfast will be also very welcome and *Punch*. In these respects I think we have it over Germany'.

By the time Sorley was ready to leave Jena on July

28th it was in a state of uproar. The assassination of the
Austrian Archduke Ferdinand by a Serb on June 28th
was at last revealing its wider implications. To begin
with only the statesmen and diplomatists of Europe
were involved, though there was a general sense of un-
easiness. But as the ultimatums grew and tension mounted,
the ordinary citizen joined in. On July 26th, when the
whole of Europe waited to learn whether Russia would
side with Serbia against Austria and Germany or not,
Sorley wrote to his parents:

> The haystack has caught fire. The drunken Verbin-
> dungen[1] are parading the streets shouting 'Down with
> the Serbs." Every half-hour, even in secluded Jena,
> comes a fresh edition of the papers, each time with
> wilder rumours: so that one can almost hear the firing
> at Belgrade. But perhaps this is only a German sab-
> batical liveliness. At any rate, it seems that Russia
> must tonight settle the question of a continental war,
> or no. Curious that an Austrian-Servian war—the one
> ideal of the late Austrian Crown-prince's life—should
> be attained first by his death.

Professor Sorley had already realized the possible course
of events and had written to both his sons, ordering them
to return to England. Kenneth dutifully obeyed, but
Charles either ignored his father's letter or had left Jena
before its arrival. Certainly he was aware of the dangers,
for on July 28th, the day he set off to meet Hopkinson
in Marburg, Austria at last declared war on Serbia. It is
more than likely that Sorley, who found the whole situation 'exciting', set out in defiance of his father's letter,
hoping for adventure. He was also unwilling to sacrifice
a walking-tour in the lovely Moselle valley.

Sorley and 'Hopper' had planned to explore the
countryside between Coblenz and Trier, an area of wood-
ed hills, lush vineyards and Roman ruins. The first four

[1] Student groups.

days were spent walking, bathing and in other more indulgent pursuits: 'Hopper was so provincial,' Sorley confided to Hutchinson, 'and, when I entered a Gasthaus with a knowing swagger and said "I wish to sample the local Mosel here; what vintage do you recommend?" Hopper would burst in with "Haben Sie Münchener Bier?" and a huge grin on his face: unwitting what a heinous sin it is to order beer in a wine district. So we generally compromized on hot milk'. Nevertheless he got on well with Hopper and spent 'three splendid days trying to make Hopper drunk with Mosel wine'.

On the fourth day, August 1st, however, when they arrived 'at the fag-end of [a] hot day's walk' in Neumagen, they were greeted by a crooked old man, who ran out at them shouting 'Der Krieg is los, Junge'.[1] Germany and England were at war and their walking-tour had abruptly ended. Sorley and Hopkinson were now officially enemy aliens, but no one seemed particularly concerned by this at Neumagen. The villagers were too bound up in their celebrations to care, and the local policeman was too kind to arrest them, as Sorley records:

> The song and guitar were busy in Neumagen all that night. 'When you get back to England,' said the fatherly policeman to me, 'you tell them that Germany doesn't sleep.' But what the lights of the street had hid, the light of day next morning showed us. It was 'quantum mutatus ab illo Hectore.'[2] The children, who seemed to scent disaster, were crying—all of those I saw. The women were mostly snuffling and gulping, which is worse. And the men, the singers of the night before, with drawn faces and forced smiles, were trying to seek comfort from their long drooping pipes and envying those who need not rejoin their barracks till Tuesday. It was Sunday, and the wailing notes of an

[1] The war has broken out, young men.
[2] 'How much changed from that Hector', *Aeneid* II, line 274.

intercession service on a bad organ were exuded from the church in the background. I have never seen a sight more miserable.

Sorley and Hopkinson decided to make for Trier by train and on arrival there gave themselves up to a military guard, who marched them off to prison as spies. 'To be exact, the "imprisonment" only lasted 8½ hours,' Sorley confessed to Hutchinson; 'but I was feeling a real prisoner by the time they let us out. I had a white cell, a bowl of soup, a pitcher of solidifying water, a hole in the wall through which I talked to the prisoner next door, a prison bed, a prison bible: so altogether they did the thing in style'. Feelings ran higher in Trier than in Neumagen and Sorley and Hopkinson were accompanied to the prison by a hostile crowd shouting: 'Shoot them! Shoot them!' Once in his cell Sorley amused himself by reading a German penny novel and talking to a 'most delightful' German prisoner through a hole in the wall. The man had been sentenced to nine months' imprisonment for remarking *sotto voce* on parade that officers were funny fellows. 'But thank God this isn't Prussia,' he concluded, 'or else it would have been two years'. He disturbed Sorley further by telling him that he was occupying a cell vacated by a Frenchman, who had been taken out and shot an hour before Sorley entered it—simply for being French. Fortunately for Sorley and Hopkinson the English were not yet regarded with such hatred and after questioning they were released and given a free pass describing them as 'unsuspicious'. Sorley took advantage of the general confusion in German minds as to which side the English had taken and encouraged a rumour that England had declared war against Russia on Germany's side. As a result the two young Englishmen were given an enthusiastic send-off by the same crowd who had hissed them on arrival.

At Trier station all was in chaos and Sorley realized

anew the tragic implications of war for ordinary people:

> . . . train after train passing crowded with soldiers
> bound for Metz: varied once or twice by a truck-load
> of "swarthier alien crews," thin old women like wine-
> skins, with beautiful and piercing faces, and big heavy
> men and tiny aged-looking children: Italian colonists
> exiled to their country again. Occasionally one of the
> men would jump out to fetch a glass of water to relieve
> their thirst in all that heat and crowding. The heat of
> the night is worse than the heat of the day, and
> geistige Getränke were verboten.[1] Then the train
> would slowly move out into the darkness that led to
> Metz and an exact reproduction of it would steam in
> and fill its place: and we watched the signal on the
> southward side of Trier, till the lights should give a
> jump and the finger drop and let in the train which
> was to carry us out of that highly-strung and thrilling
> land.

Sorley and Hopkinson eventually caught a very slow
train, which took the whole of Sunday night to reach
Cologne. There a 'sad thing' happened, Sorley told Hutchinson 'and Paul and Barnabas parted. Barnabas went on
in the same train to Amsterdam hoping thereby to reach
Hook; while Paul (ravenous for breakfast) "detrained"
at Cologne and had a huge meal. I, of course, was Paul'.
Sorley's love of food created a great many problems,
though he afterwards felt he had learnt from the experiences it brought him. At Cologne station, for instance,
he saw a group of about thirty American schoolmistresses,
whom he had helped entertain at Professor Eucken's
Sunday 'tea' only a fortnight previously. Their panic-
stricken behaviour contrasted sharply with the distress
of the natives, which impressed him as being 'quieter and
stronger and more full-bodied . . . because it was the
Vaterland and not the individual that was darting about

[1] Strong drinks were forbidden.

and looking for the way and was in need'. His imagination is even more stimulated by the 'silent submissive unquestioning faces of the dark uprooted Italians peering from the squeaking trucks' which formed a fitting background and reminded him of 'Cassandra from the backmost car looking steadily down on Agamemnon as he stepped from his triumphal purple chariot and Clytemnestra offered him her hand'.

Sorley left such scenes of desolation at Cologne to be confronted with others, for he was turned out of his train at a deserted village on the Belgian frontier and had to walk to the nearest town before he could continue on to Brussels. Once there he could find no one willing to change German money. He had to call on half the consuls in the place to solve his financial difficulties—and then travel 'sordidly' on to Antwerp. As he passed through Liège he saw nothing to suggest the strength of its defences or the proximity of the Germans. A 'Belgian soldier or two by the bridges with their helmets like tin top-hats and their uniforms resembling that of Waterloo times, alone disturbed the agricultural peace of that tract of country,' he told Hutchinson. 'Many men of military age were still at work in the fields, and the train service was running as quietly and uninterruptedly as ever'. At Antwerp he found calm of a different kind—the calm of resignation. 'The Germans will be here in twelve hours' time,' the people told him, 'they're already over the frontier.' Not even the Belgians could have anticipated the famous resistance of the Liège forces against the German army, which began two days later on August 5th and disrupted the Germans' plan for invading France.

Hopkinson had already sailed safely to Harwich by the time Sorley arrived at Antwerp to find the last boat gone:

so the English consul chartered an old broken-down

sad ship called the 'Montrose' [he wrote to Hutchinson]. It was being embalmed in Antwerp Harbour because Miss Le Neve had been taken prisoner on board it four years ago.[1] They gave us Capt. Kendall, who was last seen going down with the 'Empress of Ireland,' to take command. And after three days' journey with commercial travellers of the most revoltingly John Bullish description, I got home on Thursday . . . But mark. Hopper, who arrived triumphant at Harwich two days before I did, had to pay for his crossing. I got a free passage as far as London, where I borrowed money from my aunt's butler to take me on to Cambridge; and my aunt repaid the debt.

Sorley was sorry to find Aunt Mary out when he eventually reached her house in Onslow Square, particularly since his Belgian money was now as useless as his German money had been in Belgium. When he wrote to thank her afterwards for the hospitality he had 'demanded and taken' in her absence, he gave her a lengthy account of his adventures, which he knew she would appreciate. 'Well, I'm sorry I couldn't stay on to see you,' he concluded, 'but I think it's absolutely necessary to be back this evening, especially as I have been in a hypothetical and missing state for some time'. When he reached Cambridge on August 6th, he was in the same clothes he had worn hiking in the Moselle valley and the maid mistook him for the gardener, who usually inherited Sorley's castoffs. He was of course welcomed back with joy and relief by his anxious family and all seemed well. However, once the excitement had died down he was left facing a difficult decision—whether to enlist or not.

---

[1] Dr Crippen, the notorious murderer, and his mistress Miss Le Neve were both arrested on board the *Montrose*.

8
The Army: in Training

When Sorley returned to England in August 1914, he found a country almost hysterical with patriotic fervour and he reacted violently against it. 'But isn't all this bloody?' he asked Hutchinson, a few days after his safe arrival in Cambridge. 'I am full of mute and burning rage and annoyance and sulkiness about it. I could wager that out of twelve million eventual combatants there aren't twelve who really want it. And "serving one's country" is so unpicturesque and unheroic when it comes to the point. Spending a year in a beastly Territorial camp guarding telegraph wires has nothing poetical about it: nor very useful as far as I can see'. It is important to remember that Sorley was 'helplessly angry', as he put it, about war from the start, for it shows greater maturity and discernment than most of his contemporaries. Very few soldier-poets realized the futility of war at such an early stage. Both Rupert Brooke and Julian Grenfell have been excused their initial enthusiasm on the grounds that they did not live to see the horrors of the Somme. Yet Sorley had already realized in the first month of war many of its horrifying implications. His attitude was complicated, however, by an adventurous spirit and natural sense of decency, which made him want to fight for his country.

Sorley's reaction to the war was further complicated by his deep respect and affection for the Germans, with whom he had just spent seven happy months. 'They are a splendid lot,' he wrote defiantly to Wynne Willson, 'and I wish the silly papers would realize that they are fighting for a principle just as much as we are. If this war proves (as I think it will) that you can kill a person and yet remain his greatest friend—or, less preferably, be killed and yet stay friends—it'll have done a splendid

157

thing'. His sympathy for Germany emerges clearly in a more detailed analysis to Hopkinson:

> . . . it seems to me that Germany's only fault (and I think you often commented on it in those you met) is a lack of real insight and sympathy with those who differ from her. We are not fighting a bully, but a bigot. They are a young nation and don't yet see that what they consider is being done for the good of the world may be really being done for self-gratification . . . I regard the war as one between sisters, between Martha and Mary, the efficient and intolerant, against the casual and sympathetic. Each side has a virtue for which it is fighting, and each that virtue's supplementary vice. And I hope that whatever the material result of the conflict, it will purge these two virtues of their vices, and efficiency and tolerance will no longer be incompatible.

However sympathetic he is towards Germany Sorley realizes that he must choose between the two countries and he has no hesitation: 'But I think that tolerance is the larger virtue of the two, and efficiency must be her servant. So I am quite glad to fight this rebellious servant.'

Though greatly disturbed by the conflict his feelings for Germany aroused, Sorley could also see the humorous side to war, especially at the outset. 'Yours was the first post-card,' he told Hutchinson, 'which has come to this house in the last week which did not say "We are cutting down bacon and *so* amused trying to work out little economies. Now, what are *you* doing?"' The gravity of the situation only emphasized for Sorley certain absurdities of middle-class living, which in turn led him to even wilder fancies: if a fine were to be imposed on all those who invoked the word 'God' in connexion with the war, he believed that England's financial problems would be solved. Interjections such as 'Good God', would not be as heavily penalised as pious phrases like

'God never meant'. 'We have had so many such letters,' he concludes, 'I often think that if talking about the war were altogether forbidden it would be good. Our friends and correspondents don't seem able to give up physical luxuries without indulging in emotional luxuries as compensation. But I'm thankful to see that Kipling hasn't written a poem yet.'

In spite of such frivolities, it is quite clear that Sorley believes England must fight and that he must fight for her. He decides therefore to volunteer at once, but is not sure how to go about it. So he searches out his O.T.C. discharge report, which is marked EXCELLENT, and takes it proudly to a local official. When the man advises him to apply for a commission in the Territorials he does so, knowing that he will almost certainly get one. After a few days' reflection, however, he begins to regret his decision. 'Compromise as usual,' he writes to Hutchinson. 'Not heroic enough to do the really straight thing and join the regulars as a Tommy, I have made a stupid compromise [with] my conscience and applied for a commission in the Terriers,[1] where no new officers are wanted'. While he waits for his commission to come through his guilt increases: his comfortable existence, with its good food and rubber of bridge every evening seems a reproach. He cannot even pretend he is sacrificing a year at Oxford, since he has never been really keen to go there. Above all he cannot feel 'splendidly patriotic' like everyone else; he identifies nearly as closely with the Germans as with the English. He is further irritated by his mother's lady friends, who constantly rush up to him in the street, saying 'O, you're the boy that's had such *adventures*. Been in prison too, I hear. You *must* come and tell us all about it'. Even his aunts want a detailed account of his adventures. With his usual sense of balance Sorley begins to see the humorous side to his situation. 'I shall

[1] A 'Tommy' is a private soldier, as opposed to an officer; 'Terriers' is a nickname for members of the Territorial Army.

probably be driven,' he tells Hutchinson, 'into writing a book "Across Germany in an O.M. tie" or "Prison Life in Germany by one who has seen it," followed shortly by another entitled: "Three days on the open sea with Commercial Travellers" or "Britannia Rules the Waves".

Sorley's conscience eventually got the better of him and when the chance to join the Regular Army occurred he seized it, by applying to Oxford University Board of Military Studies on the first possible day. Another period of waiting followed and he was just about to enlist as a private when his commission came through. 'If you read the Gazette on Wednesday last,' he wrote proudly to Hutchinson at the end of August, 'you would have seen that I, even I, had been gazetted as a temporary 2nd Lieut. to the New Army (called Kitchener's Army because it doesn't belong to Kitchener any more than to me). So no Territorials for me! I'm not contented now with anything less than Regulars'.

Sorley left at once, though not to join his unit, which was the seventh battalion of the Suffolk Regiment and one of the new 'service' battalions.[1] Instead he was sent for a month's training to Churn Camp on the Berkshire downs. Little over a year before he had been there with the Marlborough O.T.C. and still remembered the lemonade and buns he had consumed in large quantities. 'But now I am visiting it under changed conditions,' he reminds himself and Hutchinson, 'and trying to attach some meaning and purpose to that hideous heap of straight-laced conventionality called drill. But otherwise it's fairly pleasant. Three in a tent and very good food—but work all day, even on the Lord's'.

To begin with Sorley is swept off his feet by the excitement of his commission, his smart uniform, his special training and his sense of being vital to the safety of his country. His mind is taken up with 'affairs of national importance', as he mockingly puts it. He is

[1] These were formed to keep communications open.

aware, however, of having succumbed to something he does not really believe in. He is almost convinced that war is right and that the tales told of German barbarism are true. He fears he has become 'non-individual and British'. Disturbed by what might be happening to him, his thoughts turn again to what he really believes in and on his way to join his battalion on the South coast in September, he tries once more to express these beliefs in verse. 'Whom Therefore We Ignorantly Worship' was sparked off at Paddington Station, where he 'refused to be so sentimental as to see the [Marlborough College] special off, but made up a sentimental poem on the way to Shorncliffe instead'. He felt it deserved a prize for being the first poem written since August 4th that was not patriotic. However, it has more to recommend it than that:

> These things are silent. Though it may be told
> Of luminous deeds that lighten land and sea,
> Strong sounding actions with broad minstrelsy
> Of praise, strange hazards and adventures bold,
> We hold to the old things that grow not old:
> Blind, patient, hungry, hopeless (without fee
> Of all our hunger and unhope are we),
> To the first ultimate instinct, to God we hold.
>
> They flicker, glitter, flicker. But we bide,
> We, the blind weavers of an intense fate,
> Asking but this—that we may be denied:
> Desiring only desire insatiate,
> Unheard, unnamed, unnoticed, crucified
> To our unutterable faith, we wait.

This sonnet is a curious mixture of technical skill and clumsiness, of Christian and pagan concepts. Parts of it are luminous in their simplicity, particularly the opening and closing phrases of each section, other parts are awkward, archaic and obscure—'without fee / of all our hunger and unhope are we'. But the thought is not easily expressed, in fact as Sorley insists his faith is 'unutterable', yet he must try to formulate it. Some of the images, such as 'crucified', suggest that he is returning to a more conventional view of religion, others suggest that he is becoming yet more pagan in his beliefs: 'We, the blind weavers of an intense fate' reminds one of his love of Greek literature and Hardy. It is also an odd anticipation of his response to Hardy's *The Dynasts*, which he starts to read two months after finishing this poem. There is the same restless almost masochistic yearning to live a harsh life devoted to the search for truth that he celebrated in 'Barbury Camp' and admired in Goethe's *Faust*. He still retains his Calvinistic suspicion of comfort and certainty:

> Asking but this—that we may be denied:
> Desiring only desire insatiate,
> Unheard, unnamed, unnoticed, crucified
> To our unutterable faith, we wait.

Sorley emphasizes his belief in the anonymity and unimportance of the individual in the whole scheme of things by repeating the negative prefix 'un—' four times in the last two lines of his sonnet. When he joins his battalion at Shorncliffe he feels even more anonymous, to begin with at least. 'Arriving six years ago at M.C., I was mocked: here I am ignored,' he complains to Hutchinson, who is still at Marlborough. 'I had to find out everything for myself, and everyone said "Ha! Don't trouble me. Trouble the Ad." I at last discovered the Ad. (the syllables jutant are not *ad*ded by the really smart). He refused to be troubled, but told me I wasn't wanted till Monday'. Sorley is provoked by Captain Gadd's indifference into replying to his off-hand questions: 'Sir, I am most efficient'. He then proceeds to prove he is not by taking the wrong platoon to Church the next day! In desperation he writes to Hutchinson: 'Well, here am

I (as Samuel put it) with my "unit" on the South Coast. You notice the word "unit". It is supremely character- istic. For the battalion *is* the unit. The component parts of it are merely quarters and fractions of it and are allow- ed no individuality at all. I am a decimal!' Once more he is moved to verse and again it takes the form of a comparison between the life of the soldier and that of the non-combatant, this time the poet:

TO POETS

We are the homeless, even as you,
Who hope and never can begin.
Our hearts are wounded through and through
Like yours, but our hearts bleed within.
We too make music, but our tones
'Scape not the barrier of our bones.

We have no comeliness like you.
We toil, unlovely, and we spin.
We start, return: we wind, undo:
We hope, we err, we strive, we sin,
We love: your love's not greater, but
The lips of our love's might stay shut.

We have the evil spirits too
That shake our soul with battle-din.
But we have an eviller spirit than you,
We have a dumb spirit within:
The exceeding bitter agony
But not the exceeding bitter cry.

Sorley presents his thoughts in a series of comparisons and contrasts, embodied in a fairly simple stanza form. By adding a couplet to a quatrain he provides himself a means of emphasizing and summarizing the main point of each verse. He links these verses together extern- ally by using the same two rhymes in the first four lines of each of the three stanzas and his increasing technical skill is shown in the way he handles this device. The simple rhythms and syntax are saved from monotony by the use of enjambement. By not specifically referring to soldiers, Sorley widens the implications of the poem to include all who lead uncreative lives (in contrast to the poets). Yet it is clear that he is thinking of the negativeness of war in general and army life in particular. As we know from earlier poems and letters, Sorley is not afraid of suffering, indeed he seems to welcome it, but he is frustrated by the vision of suffering which is not positive and which leads to destruction rather than creation. He addresses himself to poets, not as one of them, but as someone whose life has lost its creative outlet. Much of the imagery is religious and reflects another attempt to work out a moral system for himself. The concluding stanza shows that for him man is only 'evil' when he is barren and unproductive. The worst aspect of war is its effects on the *spirit* rather than the body. There is very little mention of physical suffering in Sorley's war poetry for this reason.

It is ironic that Sorley's frustration at not being able to write poetry in the army should result in such a penetrating poem. And the poem which follows the same month shows an even finer insight into the true horrors of war. Opening with a startling and nightmarish image symbolising the complete insignificance of man in the holocaust, the poem is filled with a sense of desolation and bewilderment and ends with the same powerful image which opened it:

A hundred thousand million mites we go
Wheeling and tacking o'er the eternal plain,
Some black with death—and some are white with woe.
Who sent us forth? Who takes us home again?

And there is sound of hymns of praise—to whom?
And curses—on whom curses?—snap the air.

And there is hope goes hand in hand with gloom,
And blood and indignation and despair.

And there is murmuring of the multitude
And blindness and great blindness, until some
Step forth and challenge blind Vicissitude
Who tramples on them: so that fewer come.

And nations, ankle-deep in love or hate,
Throw darts or kisses all the unwitting hour
Beside the ominous unseen tide of fate;
And there is emptiness and drink and power.

And some are mounted on swift steeds of thought
And some drag sluggish feet of stable toil.
Yet all, as though they furiously sought,
Twist turn and tussle, close and cling and coil.

A hundred thousand million mites we sway
Writhing and tossing on the eternal plain,
Some black with death—but most are bright with Day!
Who sent us forth? Who brings us home again?

The simplicity of the stanza form is matched here by
the directness of the imagery—black, white, blindness,
hymns, curses, swift steeds and bright Day. These rather
crude images which are not developed suggest the poet
feels this is no time for subtleties or sophistications.
Sorley is describing his apocalyptic vision of man's
situation which is not dissimilar to Shelley's half-
despairing, half-hopeful picture in *The Triumph of Life*.
Like Shelley Sorley has no answers to his own bewildered
questions, though he seems to see some hope in the last
stanza, where 'white with woe' is transformed to 'bright
with Day'. At the same time this phrase adds to the
sense of tragedy implicit in the probable deaths of millions of fresh young men in war. The circular movement
of the poem, which closes with a repetition of the
opening stanza in a slightly varied form, underlines the

sense of desperate, pointless movement, for in the end we seem to be back where we started. This frantic yet hopeless activity is also emphasized by the abrupt, broken rhythms and heavy alliteration of such lines as 'Twist, turn and tussle, close and cling and coil'. It is evident from both these early war poems that Sorley was suspicious of the subjective approach; he seems to feel that the excessive emotions aroused by war must be controlled by a more objective, impersonal approach to the subject. So he distances himself and his reader from the actual physical experience and everyday details, concentrating instead on more abstract but no less powerful realities.

This initial outburst of creative energy seems to have been quickly smothered by the tedious routine of army life and the attitude of his fellow-soldiers. A month after finishing his two poems Sorley writes to Hutchinson: 'I feel the lack of my usual interests pretty sharply, nothing to read all day and no time; when one thinks, one does so on the sly; and as for writing poetry in the Officers' Mess—it's almost as bold a thing as that act of God's in writing those naughty words over the wall at Belshazzar's Feast!' One of the reasons he admired the Germans was that they wrote poetry openly and would 'recite it with gusto to any three hours' old acquaintance'. While continuing to appreciate the novelty of wartime experience, he fears its eventual effects: 'It makes people think too much of the visible virtues—bravery, endurance and the obvious forms of self-sacrifice, which are noticed and given their reward of praise. It's a time of glorification of the second-best'. Sorley himself was in no danger of succumbing to such views, though he had his share of bravery, endurance and self-sacrifice, as we shall see. What·he feared most for himself was the dulling effect of army life. 'The monotony of this existence is alarming, and on the increase' he tells Kenneth, who is at Oxford, early in 1915:

Officers and men are both suffering equally from
staleness. We don't look like removing for a long time
yet on account of our supposed inefficiency. So the
passage of days is swift, and nothing to show for it.
Somehow one never lives in the future now, only in
the past, which is apt to be morbid and begins to make
one like an old man. The war is a chasm in time. I do
wish that all journalists etc., who say that war is an
ennobling purge etc., etc., could be muzzled. It simply
makes people unhappy and uncomfortable, if that is a
good thing. All illusions about the splendour of war
will, I hope, be gone after the war.

The novelty of seeing people twice his age obey him has
now passed off and the rest is 'complete stagnation
among a mass of straps and sleeping-bags and water-
bottles'. An uncharacteristic cynicism, at times even
bitterness, creeps into his letters and on 25 January 1915
he is writing to Hutchinson: 'War in England only means
putting all the men of "military age" in England into a
state of routinal coma, preparatory to getting them
killed. You are being given six months to become conventional; your peace thus made with God, you will be
sent out and killed'. In some respects he would rather
be out in France, for he finds the 'alarming sameness with
which day passes day' worse than 'any so-called atroc-
ities'. He has become less rather than more patriotic
and, correspondingly, even more sympathetic towards
the Germans, whom he believes at least to have ideals:

England—I am sick of the sound of the word. In training to fight for England, I am training to fight for that
deliberate hypocrisy, that terrible middle-class sloth
of outlook and appalling 'imaginative indolence' that
has marked us out from generation to generation.
Goliath and Caiaphas—the Philistine and the Pharisee—
pound these together and there you have Suburbia
and Westminster and Fleet Street. And yet we have

the impudence to write down Germany (who with all their bigotry are at least seekers) as 'Huns,' because they are doing what every brave man ought to do and making experiments in morality. Not that I approve of the experiment in this particular case.

Out of his conflict of feeling about Germany Sorley composes another sonnet in which he tries to reconcile the two countries, in the future if not in the present. 'To Germany' centres round the biblical image, with all its moral overtones, of the blind leading the blind:

You are blind like us. Your hurt no man designed,
And no man claimed the conquest of your land.
But gropers both through fields of thought confined
We stumble and we do not understand.
You only saw your future bigly planned,
And we, the tapering paths of our own mind,
And in each other's dearest ways we stand,
And hiss and hate. And the blind fight the blind.

When it is peace, then we may view again
With new-won eyes each other's truer form
And wonder. Grown more loving-kind and warm
We'll grasp firm hands and laugh at the old pain,
When it is peace. But until peace, the storm
The darkness and the thunder and the rain.

There is no great subtlety either of language or meaning here, in fact it is one of the least skilful of Sorley's army poems, yet the sincerity of his belief in the need for a new vision and understanding shines through clearly. As with much of his work he is far more concerned with context than technique here. It is interesting to note that whereas in earlier poems he had found God in the 'thunder and the rain', he now sees these elements as symbols of an evil time. It is as though his belief in the God of nature has been destroyed by the horrors of a situation which cannot be explained in terms of pantheism. Sorley's only hope is that war might help to destroy patriotism and all such artificial divisions. 'But all these convictions are useless for me to state,' he confesses to Hutchinson, 'since I have not had the courage of them. What a worm one is under the cart-wheels—big clumsy careless lumbering cart-wheels—of public opinion. I might have been giving my mind to fight against Sloth and Stupidity: instead, I am giving my body (by a refinement of cowardice) to fight against the most enterprising nation in the world'.

Sorley also reproached himself for not having followed his convictions and enlisted as a private soldier. He preferred physical discomfort and mental ease to the reverse, which he now suffered. 'The lower one is in rank the freer one is,' he believed, 'and it needs far more self-command to control than to obey. And I hate people with self-command'. The army system reminded him in many ways of the public school hierarchy, particularly in the matter of N.C.Os—'the N.C.O's being the prefects of the system, though with little power of individual action outside stereotyped lines'. When promoted to full lieutenant in November 1914 his reaction is similar to being made a prefect and Head of House at Marlborough: 'if I had come down to M.C.' he told Hutchinson in December, 'you'd have seen into what a state of degradation I had sunk. I wished to see you then, before you had also started the downward path which comes of having to command men. Never again in my whole life will I exercise any authority over anyone again after this war'. With his usual wit and perception he pinpointed the cause of his problem:

I am not quite one of those like that man who wrote up to the *Morning Post* Enquiry Bureau (a constant source of joy in these serious times) thus: 'Gentleman with cotton umbrella and clean habits feels he can command men. Where will he be useful? Unmarried.'

The last remark was obvious. We who are critics by
nature are somewhat out of our element commanding.

In spite of his dislike of commanding, Sorley was as
popular with his men as he had been with the younger
boys at Marlborough. He had not given up his intention
of becoming a social worker and he enjoyed this, his first
contact with working-class men. He could not help con-
trasting them favourably with the average public school
boy and, though exaggerated, his view of the ranks is
not romanticized:

The system is roughly the same: the house-master or
platoon-commander entrusts the discipline of his
charge to prefects or corporals, as the case may be.
They never open their mouths in the barrack-room
without the introduction of the unprintable swear-
words and epithets: they have absolutely no 'morality'
(in the narrower, generally accepted sense): yet the
public school boy should live among them to learn a
little Christianity: for they are so extraordinarily nice
to one another. They live in and for the present: we
in and for the future. So they are cheerful and charit-
able always: and we often niggardly and unkind and
spiteful. In the gymnasium at Marlborough, how the
few clumsy specimens are ragged and despised and
jeered at by the rest of the squad; in the gymnasium
here you should hear the sounding cheer given to the
man who has tried for eight weeks to make a long-
jump of eight feet and at last by the advice and
assistance of others has succeeded. They seem instinct-
ively to regard a man singly, at his own rate, by his
own standards and possibilities, not in comparison
with themselves or others: that's why they are so far
ahead of us in their treatment and sizing up of others.

Nevertheless Sorley's closest friends in the army were

amongst the officers. He was delighted to find on arrival at Shorncliffe that he was to be joined by another Old Marlburian: 'My only present help in trouble is—not, on this occasion, God—' he wrote to Hutchinson on 20 September 1914, 'but the knowledge that Philpott (J.R.) is arriving next Saturday in the same position as I'. He found Philpott a 'great addition', who just made the difference between him being miserable and comparatively happy. John Reginald Philpott, who was two years older than Sorley, had been in C_1 House and the Sixth with him, but left four terms earlier for Magdalen College, Oxford. When he joined the Suffolks Sorley wrote to Wynne Willson: 'we have been reinforced by that excellent fellow J.R. Philpott, who uses his old gift of apologetic satire to great advantage: so that C_1 . . . is (numerically at any rate) strongly represented'. When Philpott had to go into hospital in January 1915 Sorley's growing boredom with army life was intensified and he longed for his return. Marlborough was also represented at Shorncliffe by John Tilley, 'debonair as ever' according to Sorley who had been in a different house from him and a higher form at school: 'We are sharing an undersized mess-room, a barrack erected before the days of bathrooms, and one writing table with the Norfolk Regiment', he told Wynne Willson in October 1914: 'so that the elegant Tilley is also among my mess-mates'. Sorley had not been close friends with either Tilley or Philpott at Marlborough, yet he now became very fond of both. Looking back on his army acquaintanceships, he analyses them with his usual perception and positiveness:

They are extraordinarily close, really, these friendships of circumstance, distinct as they remain from friendships of choice. If one looks back to early September and sees what one thought of these others then; how one would never, while not disliking them, have wished to see any of them again; but that incorrigible circumstance kept us pinned together, rubbed off our odd and awkward corners where we grated: developing in each a part of himself that might have remained always unsuspected, which could tread on common ground with another. Only, I think, once or twice does one stumble across that person into whom one fits at once: to whom one can stand naked, all disclosed. But circumstance provides the second best: and I'm sure that any gathering of men will in time lead to a very close half-friendship between them all (I only say half-friendship because I wish to distinguish it from the other).

Whatever Sorley said about preferring physical to mental discomfort, another aspect of army life he enjoyed, apart from friendships, was the standard of living enjoyed by officers: 'We are like the doomed murderer at breakfast, which he has been allowed to choose before being hanged,' he joked with Wynne Willson: 'they're doing us really well'. He had to work hard, it is true, from 8.30 a.m. to 4 p.m., but he came to regard it 'as one regarded work at Marlborough, as a not at all actively disagreeable necessity, which is sooner or later certain to be over and leave a large interval of freedom before it resumes. As at Marlborough one goes through the former part passively and unsentiently, and it is only in the latter part that one lives. And as in the latter part one does not read military handbooks nor discuss tactical problems (shockingly enough) it may be said that the war abroad has hardly yet, beyond the loss of some acquaintances and an occasional anxiety for others, affected us here at all!'

This was written in November 1914 when army life in England still permitted such luxuries as rugger matches on Saturday afternoons and, even better, cross-country running. To Sorley's delight the Suffolks did very well in the divisional and garrison cross-country race which had 400 starters and 12 teams, including two battalions of the Royal Fusiliers, 'every one of whom were ex-harriers,' Sorley told Gidney. 'A heavy course over the rich Kentish soil, but the win went as it surely should, to the amateur element, to the team of a county famed for its sluggishness, and in which quoits is the favourite sport. The Suffolks came in an easy first. This has been one of our many triumphs'. Sorley had begun to grow very fond of his 'sleepy Suffolk fellows with imperturbable good tempers and an intelligent interest rather than an active co-operation in their military duties'—with which he sympathized.

In February, however, the 'sleepy' Suffolks were forced to wake up as the situation abroad deteriorated badly.[1] Sorley himself was away taking a musketry course at Hythe, when his division was suddenly ordered to Aldershot to start their Trained Soldiers' course, in preparation for France. While the Suffolks were marching twenty miles a day with packs and full equipment on, Sorley is doing very different exercises, which he finds most stimulating after months of mental lethagy:

Hythe was a restful time. I learnt and worked voraciously. After months of imperfect leadership and instruction in subjects in which oneself did not feel sure, a fortnight in which one was most magnificently and systematically spoonfed and taught, had to make shorthand notes and write exam.-papers, was a perfect mental rest-cure. The process of sitting and learning and using one's brains for assimilation of plenty (not for production and dissimulation of paucity) of knowledge was delightful to return to: as also the release from responsibility and its attendant falsities.

Sorley arrived back from Hythe to find himself in charge of an empty barracks and was forced to remain there ten days waiting for 'the advent of a wild Canadian regiment who . . . have apparently broken loose en route

[1] See page 184.

for Shorncliffe'. He spent most of his time reading Meredith's *The Egoist*. which was part of his plan to take a course of Meredith before going out to France. 'In a job like this,' he told his parents, 'it should act as Eno's Fruit Salt to the constipated brain'. After finishing *The Egoist*, he felt that Meredith like Dickens was too exaggerated and unrealistic for him, unlike Hardy whom he had also been re-reading.

Once in Aldershot Sorley joined in with the Trained Soldiers' course. Besides the usual routine of section, platoon and company drill more time was devoted to musketry and field training. The use of Lewis machine-guns, rifles, hand-grenades and mortars was also taught. Sorley, however, dismisses the Trained Soldier course rather lightly as 'a form of amusement sometimes substituted for Church on Sundays' and still cannot take the preparations for departure seriously: it has by March become 'a matter of the indifferent future to most of us,' he replies to his mother's anxious enquiries. 'If we had gone out earlier we should have gone out with a thrill in poetic-martial vein: now most of us have become by habit soldiers, at least in so far that we take such things as a matter of course and a part of our day's work that our own anticipations can neither quicken nor delay'.

Fortunately the delay in departure seems to have given Sorley the opportunity to catch up on his reading and writing. 'I have discovered a man called D.H. Lawrence who knows the way to write,' he told Hutchinson, 'and I still stick to Hardy'. He admired *The Dynasts* greatly, though he is highly critical of Hardy's more conventional war poetry, finding 'Men Who March Away' both 'arid' and 'untrue of the sentiments of the ranksmen going to war: 'Victory crowns the just' is the worst line he ever wrote—filched from a leading article in *The Morning Post*, and unworthy of him who had always previously disdained to insult Justice by offering it a material crown like victory'. He has also been reading Rupert Brooke's 1914 sonnet sequence and when Brooke dies in April 1915, Sorley can no longer contain his true feelings about him:

> I saw Rupert Brooke's death in *The Morning Post* [he writes to his mother on 28 April 1915]. *The Morning Post*, which has always hitherto disapproved of him, is now loud in his praises because he has conformed to their stupid axiom of literary criticism that the only stuff of poetry is violent physical experience, by dying on active service. I think Brooke's earlier poems— especially notably *The Fish* and *Grantchester*, which you can find in *Georgian Poetry*—are his best. That last sonnet-sequence of his, of which you sent me the review in the *Times Lit. Sup.*, and which has been so praised, I find (with the exception of that beginning 'These hearts were woven of human joys and cares, Washed marvellously with sorrow' which is not about himself) overpraised. He is far too obsessed with his own sacrifice regarding the going to war of himself (and others) as a highly intense, remarkable and sacrificial exploit, whereas it is merely the conduct demanded of him (and others) by the turn of circumstances, where the non-compliance with this demand would have made life intolerable. It was not that 'they' gave up anything of that list he gives in one sonnet: but that the essence of these things had been endangered by circumstances over which he had no control and he must fight to recapture them. He has clothed his attitude in fine words: but he has taken the sentimental attitude.

Sorley's outburst against Brooke is significant on several counts. It indicates clearly that his own aims in poetry are entirely different and, more importantly, that he saw more lucidly than Brooke from the beginning the self-deception involved in volunteering. In other words,

Sorley has no illusions about himself or the war. He is fighting largely out of self-interest for ends which he finds at best dubious. And it is this honest, intelligent and direct approach to the essential problems of war that make his next batch of poems so remarkable, particularly in the pre-Somme period of 1915.

Sorley sent these seven poems to his mother, together with his criticism of Brooke, on April 28th. 'You will notice,' he warned her, 'that most of what I have written is as hurried and angular as the handwriting: written at different times and dirty with my pocket: but I have had no time for the final touch nor seem likely to have for some time, and so send them as they are. Nor have I had the time to think out (as I usually do) a rigorous selection, as fit for other eyes'. Most of the awkwardnesses in Sorley's war poems must be excused on these grounds, but few of them justify his belief that there has been 'a fall in quality'. The war has sharpened rather than dulled his vision and, imperfect as some of them are, these later poems are superior to his schoolboy productions. However, they are not all directly concerned with war. As we have seen Sorley preferred, where possible, to distance himself from the actual event, whilst retaining its psychological truth. The first of these poems 'Deus Loquitur' is so oblique in its reference to war that at first one doubts its relevance at all. After a careful reading of this curious monologue, in which Sorley imagines himself as God surveying wayward man, it seems to suggest that in wartime God criticizes men because they return to Him in desperation rather than love:

> That's what I am: a thing of no desire,
> With no path to discover and no plea
> To offer up, so be my altar fire
> May burn before the hearth continuously,
> To be
> For wayward men a steadfast light to see.

They know me in the morning of their days,
But ere noontide forsake me, to discern
New lore and hear new riddles. But moonrays
Bring them back footsore, humble, bent, a-burn
To turn
And warm them by my fire which they did spurn.

They flock together like tired birds. 'We sought
Full many stars in many skies to see,
But ever knowledge disappointment brought.
Thy light alone, Lord, burneth steadfastly.'
Ah me!
Then it is I who fain would wayward be.

Sorley had been re-reading Browning, whose objectivity
had converted him back to him: 'since then I have used
no other,' he admitted to Wynne Willson, who had
defended Browning against Sorley at Marlborough. 'I
wish we could recall him from the stars and get him to
write a Dramatic Idyll or something, giving a soliloquy
of the feelings and motives and quick changes of heat
and cold that must be going through the poor Kaiser's
mind at present. He would really show that impartial
sympathy for him, which the British press and public so
doltishly deny him, when in talk and comment they deny
him even the rights of a human being'. Since he cannot
recall Browning from the dead, however, Sorley appears
to have tried his methods, in his choice of a dramatic
monologue, with its colloquial opening and even more
startling twist at the end, where God Himself seems tired
of His own perfection. Like Browning, too, Sorley experiments with rhythm and verse form, using the brief fifth
line of each stanza as a turning point in the thought. He
also uses a mixture of colloquial and archaic language
similar to that found in 'Fra Lippo Lippi' and 'Rabbi
Ben Ezra'.

Sorley obviously finds the dramatic monologue helpful in his search for a more objective technique and

greater impartiality, since he uses it again in his next poem, 'Brand', the first of 'Two Songs from Ibsen's Dramatic Poems'. In his choice of the young and uncompromising clergyman who sacrifices all for his convictions but is punished in the end for his lack of love, Sorley is clearly continuing his religious debate with himself. He also seems to be implying that one possible cause of war is Man's rejection of Christ, to Whom Brand addresses himself:

> I think that thou wast I in bygone places
> In an intense eliminated year.
> Now born again in days that are more drear
> I wander unfulfilled: and see strange faces.

The importance of love as part of any truly religious belief is brought out again in 'Peer Gynt', the second of the 'Two Songs from Ibsen's Dramatic Poems'. There may also be, in the person of Peer Gynt, an implied comparison between the high-spirited soldier marching out to war and the tired and wounded veteran returning defeated:

> When he was young and beautiful and bold
> We hated him, for he was very strong.
> But when he came back home again, quite old,
> And wounded too, we could not hate him long.
>
> For kingliness and conquest pranced he forth
> Like some high-stepping charger bright with foam.
> And south he strode and east and west and north
> With need of crowns and never need of home.
>
> Enraged we heard high tidings of his strength
> And cursed his long forgetfulness. We swore
> That should he come back home some eve at length,
> We would deny him, we would bar the door!
>
> And then he came. The sound of those tired feet!
> And all our home and all our hearts are his,

Where bitterness, grown weary, turns to sweet,
And envy, purged by longing, pity is.

And pillows rest beneath the withering cheek,
And hands are laid the battered brows above,
And he whom we had hated, waxen weak,
First in his weakness learns a little love.

The same mixture of irony and pity characterizes most of Sorley's war poetry. It varies from the heavy irony of 'Peer Gynt' to the almost imperceptible irony of 'All the Hills and Vales Along', undoubtedly one of his best war poems. In fact the irony here is so subtle that, contrary to all we know of Sorley's views, it has been interpreted as a straight glorification of valour and comradeship. Yet it is quite clear from the start that Sorley is relying on irony to keep his distance from the subject, which might otherwise become mawkish and sentimental. The pity of decay is brought out through a comparison between the splendours of nature and youth, which is undercut by an implicit contrast between the continuity of nature and the abrupt cutting off of the youth in their prime:

All the hills and vales along
Earth is bursting into song,
And the singers are the chaps
Who are going to die perhaps.
O Sing, marching men,
Till the valleys ring again.
Give your gladness to earth's keeping,
So be glad, when you are sleeping.

Cast away regret and rue,
Think what you are marching to.
Little live, great pass
Jesus Christ and Barabbas
Were found the same day.
This dies, that went his way.
So sing with joyful breath,

For why, you are going to death.
Teeming earth will surely store
All the gladness that you pour.

It is possible to interpret these stanzas as a sincere
expression of belief in redemption through death, that
the soldiers will live on in nature. The next two stanzas,
however, suggest that Sorley has found an answer to his
religious search neither in Pantheism ('Earth that bore
with joyful ease / Hemlock for Socrates'), nor in conventional Christianity, though he accepts the paradox of
living. And the men's fate is no longer referred to
euphemistically as 'sleeping', but baldly as 'dead'.

Earth that never doubts nor fears,
Earth that knows of death, not tears,
Earth that bore with joyful ease
Hemlock for Socrates.
Earth that blossomed and was glad
'Neath the cross that Christ had,
Shall rejoice and blossom too
When the bullet reaches you.
    Wherefore, men marching
    On the road to death, sing!
    Pour your gladness on earth's head,
    So be merry, so be dead.

From the hills and valleys earth
Shouts back the sound of mirth,
Tramp of feet and lilt of song
Ringing all the road along.
All the music of their going,
Ringing swinging glad song-throwing,
Earth will echo still, when foot
Lies numb and voice mute.
    On, marching men, on
    To the gates of death with song.
    Sow your gladness for earth's reaping,

So you may be glad, though sleeping.
Strew your gladness on earth's bed,
So be merry, so be dead.

In spite of these obvious reservations about war, the swinging, joyous rhythms show that Sorley could also respond to the excitement of the occasion and the appeal of a troop of fresh young soldiers bursting into song as they march along. It is not hard to imagine him striding along with his men through the Surrey countryside on their route marches, the very marches which are to prepare them for probable death in France. The poem is essentially ambiguous, reflecting an ambiguity of attitude. Sorley is at his best when he is groping for an answer to the enigma of war and both the rhythms and the stanza form show a skill and sophistication unequalled in earlier works. The syncopation of the compelling rhythms save them from monotony and the gradual lengthening of the stanza form, by two lines each time, reflect an enlargement of the thought.

It is clear from this and other of his army poems that Sorley has been provoked by the moral issues raised by war to try out different religious answers for himself. This would account for such puzzling poems as 'Expectans Expectavi', if Professor Sorley was right in placing this among the later poems.[1]

Like his heroes Faust and Peer Gynt, Sorley is searching for an answer to the riddle of the Universe, but he quite certainly does not find it in Christianity—the mediocrity of the verse in 'Expectans' alone shows that he is forcing his piety into false moulds.

In 'If I Have Suffered Pain' Sorley develops the idea of Faustian man searching restlessly for truth, and suffering because he refuses to 'cease / From striving and from cry'. He raises that favourite Calvinist problem of Free-will; and his answer is decisive—Man is free to choose and

[1] See pages 86-7.

this only is his compensation:

> If I have suffered pain
> It is because I would.
> I willed it. 'Tis no good
> To murmur or complain.
> I have not served the law
> That keeps the earth so fair
> And gives her clothes to wear,
> Raiment of joy and awe.

By extension, it might be argued that Man is free to fight or not and that his suffering in war is therefore the result of his own choice. This is one way of resolving the problem: if God is merciful, why must Man suffer? He does so because he is blessed with free-will, which he abuses. But as in 'Expectans' one feels that Sorley is forcing himself to accept arguments he does not really believe and the poetry suffers. The rhythms are too certain, there is little or no tension either in the content or technique and the conclusion is too pat:

> You see, the earth is bound.
> You see, the man is free.
> For glorious liberty
> He suffers and would die.
> Grudge not then suffering
> Or chastisemental cry.
> O let his pain abound,
> Earth's truant and earth's king!

Sorley has for the moment lost sight of the complexity of the questions he has been asking himself since war started eight months earlier. It is a relief to find signs of his perception and subtlety returning in his favourite poem of the batch—'Le Revenant'. The subject matter, of the returning stranger, is anticipated to some extent in 'Peer Gynt', but the handling of it is less predictable in this later poem. The protagonist—who is, by his own admission, Sorley himself—is more akin to Ulysses than Peer Gynt. He is not treated with either hostility or pity when he returns home, but worse—he has been forgotten. Sorley sublimates his longing for the Marlborough downs in the opening description of his favourite landscape, which he has not seen for more than a year:

> He trod the oft-remembered lane
> (Now smaller-seeming than before
> When first he left his father's door
> For newer things), but still quite plain
>
> (Though half-benighted now) upstood
> Old landmarks, ghosts across the lane
> That brought the Bygone back again:
> Shorn haystacks and the rooky wood;
>
> The guide post, too, which once he clomb
> To read the figures: fourteen miles
> To Swindon, four to Clinton Stiles,
> And only half a mile to home: . . .

Sorley is to bring this same signpost in, to greater effect, in a later poem and it is interesting to see him first exploring the image here.

'Le Revenant' was the last poem Sorley wrote in England, for in May 1915 his brigade was ordered to France. As they sat waiting for final instructions he was even more conscious of a split in his experience, as though he were leading two lives. On the one hand there was his intellectual life—reading books, writing poetry when he could and seeing an occasional play on leave in London. Overshadowing this, however, was the seemingly pointless round of duties and, even worse, the endless delays of army life. On 23 May 1915 he wrote in exasperation to his Jena friend, Arthur Watts:

We are in a mass of accounts I do not understand, and sometime next week we shall exchange this bloody 'area' for a troop-ship at Southampton, and then a prim little village in France in the middle of some mildly prosperous cultivation—probably. On the other hand we may sit here for weeks, making our wills and looking at our first field dressings and reading our religions on our identity discs. In jedem Falle we know that we are stale to the moulding point and sooner or later must be chucked across to France. We profess no interest in our work; our going has lost all glamour in adjournment; a weary acceptance of the tyranny of discipline, and the undisguised boredom we feel toward one another, mark all our comings and goings: we hate our general, our C.O. and men; we do not hate the Germans: in short we are nearing the attitude of regular soldiers to the army in general.

There had been talk of leaving for France since January, when the Suffolks had proved too inefficient and their departure had been postponed till March. It was not until the end of May that they finally left. By this time the Allies were suffering from a severe shortage of men. In January 1915 British troops had been sent out to Gallipoli in response to an appeal from Russia. In the Middle East British and Indian soldiers, having beaten off a Turkish attack on the Suez canal, were preparing to invade Palestine and another expeditionary force from India was fighting for possession of Baghdad. Allied attacks at Neuve Chapelle, Aubers and Festubert on the Western front caused a further dramatic reduction in numbers in the first half of 1915. Finally the German offensive at Ypres in April and May made the need for fresh troops desperate.

By the time the 7th Suffolks of the 12th Division left to help fill this gap even the most patriotic had lost their enthusiasm. Sorley, who had never felt it to begin with, was completely disillusioned. Even his initial belief in the necessity to fight the Germans on principle seems to have left him by the time he goes out to face them in battle. 'I do wish that people would not deceive themselves by talk of a just war,' he wrote to his mother. 'There is no such thing as a just war. What we are doing is casting out Satan by Satan'. It was with this attitude of complete disillusionment that Sorley now faced the prospect of almost certain death in France.

9
The Army: at the Front

When Sorley arrived in France on 30 May 1915 the Germans and Allies had reached a stalemate on the Western Front. German victories on the Belgian and Russian borders had been counterbalanced by French and British successes on the Marne. Both sides had managed to rush troops to the sea in the north and the Swiss border in the south, thus covering their flanks, so that the only hope of a rapid victory was to break through the enemy's line. All possible methods were used—bombardment with heavy artillery, surprise raids and mines. In April, the month before Sorley arrived, the Germans at the battle of Ypres had started to use poison gas on the unprepared Allies and only fear of their own weapon prevented a major breakthrough. Each time an attack was repulsed trenches were dug and the stalemate increased—'an unromantic sitting still 100 yards from Brother Bosch', Sorley called it.

Yet to begin with Sorley was highly stimulated by the situation. Nothing could have been more thrilling, he felt, than the way his Brigade had been crossed over: the first battalion left Aldershot at five one evening and the whole Brigade was in France by midnight. After two hours in an oily troopship and ten in a grimy train, which shrieked through the desolate northern plains, it was incredible to find himself arriving at dawn in a hamlet of four large farms surrounded by plane trees and fields of rye.

> But this is perfect [he wrote to Watts the following day]. The other officers have heard the heavy guns and perhaps I shall soon. They make perfect cider in this valley: still, like them. There are clouds of dust along the roads, and in the leaves: but the dust here is

native and caressing and pure, not like the dust of
Aldershot, gritted and fouled by motors and thousands
of feet. 'Tis a very Limbo lake: set between the tire-
less railways behind and twenty miles in front the
fighting. Drink its cider and paddle in its rushy streams:
and see if you care whether you die tomorrow?

This is only one of a number of lyrical outbursts from
Sorley, who found life in the little hamlet like a picnic.
As he drank its cider, ate its fresh vegetables and slept
soundly in an old four-poster bed, he began to discover
a sensual side to his nature which surprised him, though
it had emerged earlier in his love of food, the feel of rain
on bare skin and other strong physical sensations. 'It
brings out a new part of one's self, the loiterer,' he told
Watts, 'neither scorning nor desiring delights, gliding
listlessly through the minutes from meal-time to meal-
time, like the stream through the rushes: or stagnant and
and smooth like their cider, unfathomably gold: beautiful
and calm without mental fear'.

Coexisting with the sense of great tranquility is Sorley's
consciousness of danger and death. Although living in
almost complete isolation from the rest of the battalion
among quiet fields, where his men help the French-
women with the farmwork, he knows that he will soon
have to leave for the front, less than twenty miles away.
On June 8th, only a week after his arrival, he is reporting
to his father: 'We have heard no more than the distant
rumbling of the guns, but move slowly up in their direction
tomorrow'. By June 11th D Company have joined their
battalion nearer the front at Ploegsteert, 'a town of
single-line tramways and mean streets,' according to
Sorley, 'four-foot square vegetable gardens, where plain-
tive lettuces wither: cobbles, tenements, and cats that
walk on tiles'. The Franco-Flemish population is very
welcoming, however, and the women remind Sorley
of the Scots peasantry in 'their openness, initiative and

fussy motherliness'. Sorley knows that at any moment
he and his fellow-officers are likely to be sent for a
'course' in the trenches, attached to some other battalion.
He has also heard that both the first and second battalions
of his Division have already been wiped out. It is not
surprising that his thoughts turn constantly to death.
The peaceful hours spent censoring letters, finding billets
and provisions for the men 'will have slipt over me,' he
tells Watts, 'and I shall march hotly to the firing-line, by
turn critic, actor, hero, coward and soldier of fortune:
perhaps even for a moment Christian, humble, with "Thy
will be done." Then shock, combustion, the emergence
of one of these: death or life'. After less than two weeks
in France, before he has seen anything of the fighting,
Sorley is moved to write two of his best war-poems—on
death. And for this highly emotional subject he chooses
the sonnet, one of the most disciplined of forms. The
first of these 'Two Sonnets' is divided quite conventionally into an octet, in which he sets out and develops his
theme through the image of that same signpost he used
earlier in 'Le Revenant'. He extends this image in the
sestet to an unexpected conclusion—that in some ways
he looks forward to death as an adventure:

> Saints have adored the lofty soul of you.
> Poets have whitened at your high renown.
> We stand among the many millions who
> Do hourly wait to pass your pathway down.
> You, so familiar, once were strange: we tried
> To live as of your presence unaware.
> But now in every road on every side
> We see your straight and steadfast signpost there.
>
> I think it like that signpost in my land,
> Hoary and tall, which pointed me to go
> Upward, into the hills, on the right hand,
> Where the mists swim and the winds shriek and blow,

A homeless land and friendless, but a land
I did not know and that I wished to know.

It is significant that Sorley first entitled this poem
'Death on the Downs', for in it he recaptures something
of the mystery, fear and excitement of being on the
Marlborough downs in the mist, which in turn reflects
his ambivalent attitude towards death. For he both fears
and welcomes an event which may lead to the heart of
the mystery of existence. The signpost itself is based on
an actual signpost on the Marlborough downs, which he
had possibly been tempted but afraid to follow 'Upwards,
into the hills'. Though he seems to imply a belief in an
after-life, there is no suggestion of a Christian interpretation of death, as an entry to Heaven or Hell, but a more
elemental belief that it is a journey—Shakespeare's 'un-
discovered country from whose bourn no traveller returns'. The long drawn-out tension of expecting death,
without knowing when, is skilfully conveyed in the long
vowels, alliteration and assonance of the fourth line: 'Do
hourly wait to pass your pathway down'. The abrupt
juxtaposition of the fifth: 'You, so familiar, once were
strange . . .' reminds us of the speed at which this change
has taken place once Sorley is at the Front.

In his second sonnet Sorley develops the idea of the
familiarity of Death in wartime and the attraction of a
chance to start again, with a 'slate rubbed clean'. By
using this and another ordinary domestic metaphor, a
bucket, he tries to avoid romanticizing death as he feels
Rupert Brooke has done, continuing the schoolroom
metaphor even in the second more elevated part of the
poem with a 'big blot', two more powerful monosyllables,
to show the irrevocability of Death. However, in the
last three lines he does not hesitate to point out the true
pathos and glory of an early death, partly through the
transformation of 'withered' to 'stirs, rises, opens and
grows sweet / And blossoms . . .':

Such, such is Death: no triumph: no defeat:
Only an empty pail, a slate rubbed clean,
A merciful putting away of what has been.

And this we know: Death is not Life effete,
Life crushed, the broken pail. We who have seen
So marvellous things know well the end not yet.

Victor and vanquished are a-one in death:
Coward and brave: friend, foe. Ghosts do not say
'Come, what was your record when you drew breath?'
But a big blot has hid each yesterday
So poor, so manifestly incomplete.
And your bright Promise, withered long and sped,
Is touched, stirs, rises, opens and grows sweet
And blossoms and is you, when you are dead.

The sonnet form has here been given an unusual turn by
its division into two short stanzas of three lines each and
a long concluding octet, with the three parts linked by
an intricate rhyme scheme which includes half-rhyme.
The abrupt opening monosyllables suggest a direct
approach to the subject borne out by the use of the
word 'Death', rather than a euphemism. Contrast is used
throughout to suggest first that death cannot be defined
by easy extremes—'no triumph: no defeat', then that
death is a leveller, making all men equal—'Victor and
vanquished . . . coward and brave: friend, foe'—and that
even war becomes insignificant in the face of death. The
poem can be read as Sorley's attempt to formulate a
philosophy of living which will help him to face the daily
possibility of dying. On the Western Front he is learning,
as Unamuno put it, to 'live in the thought of death'.

Sorley found time to write poetry in France because,
to begin with at least, there was very little to do. Although
by the middle of June he was in the trenches for the
customary eight days, with four days in reserve, he felt
his exertions were 'those of the navvy rather than those

of the soldier'. One day, he told Kenneth, 'a man will invent automatic entrenching tools and automatic mowing machines, which will take the place of infantry in war. For the present one would have thought a spiked wall might have been erected along the British front, with several spiked walls behind in case the first got shattered, and these would do the job as efficiently as we: and would probably stand a bombardment better'. All he has seen of war so far is a cornfield, which at first seemed to be an ordinary cornfield until he noticed a long narrow trench at either end protected with barbed wire. 'You might watch that field all day,' he told his sister, 'and if you were deaf, you would never guess that both of these trenches were filled with foes: you would wonder how those queer underground inhabitants spent their time, and why they dared not show their heads above ground'. As he and his fellow-soldiers waited for the next great advance in the Loos area to the south of them, he felt even more aimless than he had in England— and as critical. 'There is no news,' he wrote in answer to Watts's queries on June 16th:

A large amount of organized disorderliness, killing the spirit. A vagueness and a dullness everywhere: an unromantic sitting still 100 yards from Brother Bosch. There's something rotten in the state of something. One feels it but cannot be definite of what. Not even is there the premonition of something big impending: gathering and ready to burst. None of that feeling of confidence, offensiveness, "personal ascendancy," with which the reports so delight our people at home. Mutual helplessness and lassitude, as when two boxers who have battered each other crouch dancing two paces from each other, waiting for the other to hit. Improvised organization, with its red hat, has muddled out romance. It is not the strong god of the Germans— that makes their Prussian Beamter so bloody and

their fight against fearful odds so successful.[1] Our
organization is like a nasty fat old frowsy cook dressed
up in her mistress's clothes: fussy, unpopular, and up-
start: trailing the scent of the scullery behind her. In
periods of rest we are billeted in a town of sewage
farms, mean streets, and starving cats: delightful population: but an air of late June weariness. For Spring
again! This is not Hell as I hoped, but Limbo Lake
with green growths on the water, full of minnows.

A week later he is complaining to Kenneth that there is
a 'very great sense of desultoriness everywhere. I believe
I meant to say sultriness, but desultoriness will do just
as well'. He feels that they have all taken root, like trees—
'and like trees we vegetate'. After a month in France he
is convinced that the time has been wasted in tedious
preparations for possibilities which will never occur.

Sorley lays the blame for the delay on the political
crisis in England, in which Lord Fisher had resigned
from the Admiralty and Winston Churchill had been
transferred from it. When a coalition government was
formed on 25 May 1915, Sorley predicts that it would
'ultimately prove to please both sides or neither, with
the odds on it doing the latter'. The war, he believes, was
being 'held over until visits from Cabinet Ministers and
Labour leaders shall have ceased'. There were other more
immediate reasons for delay, however. German defence
works in the Loos and Lens area south of Ploegsteert
were formidable, including as they did a network of
machine-gun redoubts and steel-domed forts with multiple
quick-firing guns and dug-outs, wired for electricity and
equipped with periscopes. Before attacking it was essential
that the Allies should reinforce their own defences, so
most of the hot, wet summer was spent digging, drain-
ing and flooring trenches, erecting barbed wire fences
and making simple bombs.

[1] Beamter: an official.

Sorley takes refuge from the monotony of this routine in books. His mother sends him at his request his two favourites—Jefferies' *Life of the Fields* and Goethe's *Faust* 'He reads Jefferies to remind him of Liddington Castle 'and the light green and dark green of the Aldbourne Downs in Summer'. For as his first sonnet on death showed, his thoughts turn more and more to the place where he first found meaning in life. It was in *Faust* that he found this meaning embodied in the legend of a restless spirit searching for truth. The nearer the fighting, the more he identifies with Faust. The war has released him from trivialities, in spite of the daily pettiness of army life. He finds his thoughts turning either to the past, or to the future. He tries to explain to Watts, who has replaced Hutchinson as his confidant, how army life has in some curious way freed his spirit. Instead of the conventional three years at Oxford, following his conventional public school education, he finds himself in a completely unpredictable situation. He now dreams of a future in which Watts figures as Odysseus and Sorley as his comrade in a roaming, gypsy-like existence. 'Give me *The Odyssey*,' he concludes, 'and I return the New Testament to store'.

Sorley very much regretted that he had not brought his *Odyssey* with him, for he also identifies with Ulysses, particularly now that he is preparing to fight. As the tension mounts at the beginning of July he tries to express his feeling of anticipation in a verse letter to the 'Marlborough Laureate' he so admires, John Bain:

> I have not brought my Odyssey
> With me here across the sea;
> But you'll remember, when I say
> How, when they went down Sparta way,
> To sandy Sparta, long ere dawn
> Horses were harnessed, rations drawn,
> Equipment polished sparkling bright,

And breakfasts swallowed (as the white
Of Eastern heavens turned to gold)—
The dogs barked, swift farewells were told.
The sun springs up, the horses neigh,
Crackles the whip thrice—then away!

Identifying John Bain with the Greek bard, he argues
that the meaning of war only becomes clear to men
through the interpretation of the poets:

And you our minstrel, you our bard,
Who makes war's grievous and hard,
Lightsome and glorious and fair
Will be, at least in spirit, there.
We'll read your rhymes, and we will sing
The toun o' touns till the roofs ring.
And if you'll come among us, then
We shall be most blest of men,
We shall forget the old old pain,
Remember Marlborough again
And hearken all the tales you tell
And bless our old ἀοιδός.

Sorley's nostalgia for Marlborough also comes out in a
long descriptive passage on that 'red-capped town' and
its surroundings, in which the signpost, symbol for him
of the road to adventure and possibly death, again plays
an important part:

Perhaps the road up Ilsley way,
The old ridge-track, will be my way.
High up among the sheep and sky
Look down on Wantage, passing by,
And see the smoke from Swindon town;
And then full left at Liddington,
Where the four winds of heaven meet
The earth-blest traveller to greet.
And then my face is toward the south,
There is a singing on my mouth:

194

Away to rightward I descry
My Barbury ensconced in sky,
Far underneath the Ogbourne twins,
And at my feet the thyme and whins,
The grasses with their little crowns
Of gold, the lovely Aldbourne downs,
And that old signpost (well I knew
That crazy signpost, arms askew,
Old mother of the four grass ways).

Sorley had been reading Bain's epitaphs in the *Marlburian* on boys not much older than himself already killed in the war, which reminds him once again of his own probable fate when the fighting starts.

At the end of his long verse letter to Bain Sorley apologises for it—'rough, / Jingling and tedious enough'— and when Mrs Sorley writes to suggest publishing a small collection of his poems, he refuses for this and other reasons: 'The proposal is premature: also I have at present neither the opportunity nor inclination for a careful revision and selection. Besides, this is no time for olive-yards and vineyards; more especially of the small holdings type. For three years or the duration of the war, let be'.

Another poem which survives from July 1915 suggests that Sorley was right not to publish without revision. Although interesting as a record of his feelings and his attempt to work out a philosophy, it has not the tautness of his two sonnets on death, which were written in greater leisure. The poem starts well, however, with a reflection on Man's position in the scheme of things: once again the setting is the Marlborough downs:

There is such change in all those fields,
Such motion rhythmic, ordered, free,
Where ever-glancing summer yields
Birth, fragrance, sunlight, immanency,
To make us view our rights of birth.
What shall we do? How shall we die?

We, captives of a roaming earth,
'Mid shades that life and light deny.
Blank summer's surfeit heaves in mist;
Dumb earth basks dewy-washed; while still
We whom Intelligence has kissed
Do make us shackles of our will.
And yet I know in each loud brain,
Round-clamped with laws and learning so,
Is madness more and lust of strain
Than earth's jerked godlings e'er can know.

This was the last poem Sorley sent home, apart from an epitaph on a school-friend, for towards the middle of July his battalion took over a new system of trenches. 'So all day there is trench duty broken by feverish letter censoring,' he told his mother. The 7th Suffolks were not yet at the front, but even in reserve a little excitement was provided by patrolling the enemy's barbed wire defences at night. But there was still no real fighting, for reasons which Sorley explained to his mother:

All patrols—English and German—are much averse to the death and glory principle; so, on running up against one another in the long wet rustling clover, both pretend that they are Levites and the other is a Good Samaritan—and pass by on the other side, no word spoken. For either side to bomb the other would be a useless violation of the unwritten laws that govern the relations of combatants permanently within a hundred yards of distance of each other, who have found out that to provide discomfort for the other is but a roundabout way of providing it for themselves: until they have their heads banged forcibly together by the red-capped powers behind them, whom neither attempts to understand. Meanwhile weather is 'no bon': food, 'plenty bon': temper, fair, sleep, jamais.

The strain of trench-duty was relieved by a few days' rest, spent in a small village only a kilometre behind the lines. One of the farms there reminded Sorley of Nanny Porter's parents' farm, he told her in a letter thanking her for cigarettes—'same little garden and everything—but smashed alas to ruins'. There were other reminders of war, especially in the evening when the night-raids started only a kilometre away. In a brilliant descriprive passage, written at his father's request, Sorley captures the noises in a series of unusual images. The quickfirer sounds like a cow coughing, the machine-guns like a motor-bike race; there is a noise like several express trains, which ends in a 'tremendous railway accident'. In a wilder burst of fancy he imagines a *buffalo* coughing, someone sliding down the stairs on a tin tray, and beating the tray with a broom; and finally a ring-master cracking his whip at the circus, which illuminates the sky with its firework display. Image is linked with image and developed to produce a piece of prose almost as fine as Sorley's best poems. There is no doubt that his prose style has developed during his stay in Germany and his ten months in the army.

Sorley continues to visit and return from the trenches 'with an almost monotonous regularity' throughout July but at the end of this month something happens to break the routine and to give him his first real chance to show his mettle. Sorley himself, an essentially modest person, does not report the incident to his parents, but a brother-offifer does:

We were holding trenches just to the south of Ploeg-steert wood. D Coy were on the left of the Battalion, about 100 yards from the Germans. That opposite C[harles] 's platoon was, I think, the most interesting part of our line, as the Germans were working on it from the day we took over till the day we left. They seemed to be making a redoubt of some kind, and, as those were the days when shells were scarce, we couldn't ask the gunners to blow it up. . . . C. knew the ground in front of this better than anyone in the company: where the ditches and disused saps ran, where the different shell-holes lay; where the beetroot met the clover, and where the clover ended in a strip of long thin grass up to the enemy's wire. C. had been out crawling often before, just for the fun of the thing. . . . It was all planned out cleverly beforehand: C. and three other bombers to crawl up to within bombing distance, he leading and directing the show; four riflemen were to come up on the flank and cover their retirement. . . . It was a dark night and everything went off splendidly up to the point where the bombs were to be thrown. . . . The pins had all been taken out and the second signal was just being passed when the third bomber dropped his infernal machine. I think the others heard it thud and tried to get clear; at any rate he was stupid enough to fumble about in the long wet grass in an attempt to find it. There was a dreadful five seconds' suspense: then the thing exploded right under him. In the confusion C. and one of the other men managed to throw their bombs, and that and the fire of the riflemen, who opened up a steady burst immediately, saved the party somewhat. C. crawled to the man who had dropped his bomb and dragged him into the shell-hole. . . . The shell-hole was his salvation. They had only just got into it when the Germans swept the ground with an absolute hail of rifle and machine-gun fire and lit up all around with Véry lights. . . . When the Germans had quieted down a bit, some more men came out and helped to get the wounded in. The one with C. was in a very bad way and died soon after. C. said every bone in the upper part of his body must have been broken—it was like carrying a piece of living pulp—and he never forgot the curious inarticulate cry of the man as he picked him up. . . .

Next morning, a brilliant July day, I went round to pick up Intelligence and met C. on trench patrol. He had just come from breakfasting and was dressed in summer get-up; gum boots, breeches, shirt-sleeves, sambrown belt and pistol. He had a bandage round his head, but only a very slight scratch from a fragment of bomb. He was walking along, reading from his German pocket edition of *Faust*. He told me the whole story of the raid: rather sorry that his plans had been let down just when they might have been so successful; but he took it all in his happy careless fashion.

It is clear from this account that Sorley was not only ingenious, but also cool-headed and courageous in the face of danger. Like most brave men, he was an unwilling hero and confessed quite openly his horror of such deeds as rescuing a dying man. In spite of several tests of his courage, Sorley still feared he might fail at the moment of crisis. It was not for another two months, however, that Sorley was put to the ultimate test. For the stalemate dragged on through August and though the 7th Suffolks were very busy there were still only occasional skirmishes at night to try their courage. Sorley was forced to admire the 'unfathomable laboriousness' of the Germans, 'infinite and aloof! Working day and night, not heeding us'. He saw the British as 'a gnat that buzzes, hums and stings without ceasing' but the Germans as 'the bee, undisturbable in toil, till roused, and then a deep sting which remains'. Though the casualties rose throughout August, the 7th had lost very few officers and Sorley still felt reasonably secure. He started to look forward to leave but at the end of August he was promoted to captain and his leave was changed from mid-September to mid-October. He was now second-in-command of D Company. His promotion had come about because the commander of D Company, Captain C.H. Turner, had been promoted to major and given command of the 2nd Suffolks. Sorley's job was with money and business affairs and he felt it was a useful move, since it gave him an opportunity to master accountancy. Another quite different task he had taken on was the running of a large public-house—'buying barrels of beer direct from neighbouring brewers and selling it as nearly as possible at cost price to the men,' he explained to his father, 'thus saving them from the adulterated and expensive beer at the local estaminets'. With the profit he bought mouth-organs and suet for the men—'the Suffolks love of suet pudding being as great almost as his love of sleep'.

In the same letter, and less lightheartedly, Sorley writes 'Reading the casualty lists each morning I feel thankful our division was not sent to the Dardanelles'. After months of unsuccessful attempts to capture the Gallipoli Peninsula, the British had launched another attack in Suvla Bay, but were suffering heavy casualties. It was not long, however, before Sorley's own regiment and many others in the Loos area began to suffer equally heavy losses. For on September 25th, only three weeks after Sorley wrote these words, the British First Army, supported by the French Ninth Army, launched a new attack on the Hohenzollen redoubt to the north of Loos. On September 30th Sorley, with his battalion, had been moved from Ploegsteert to a chalk pit in the battle area which had been captured by the Coldstream Guards in the main attack. Almost immediately they were subjected to a violent artillery bombardment, during which they lost numbers of men, including their divisional commander, Major-General Wing. As they waited to join in the main attack on 5 October 1915, Sorley wrote to Wynne Willson with his usual positive attitude towards all experience, however unpleasant:

The chess players are no longer waiting so infernal long between their moves. And the patient pawns are all in movement, hourly expecting further advances—whether to be taken or reach the back lines and be queened. 'Tis sweet, this pawn-being: there are no cares, no doubts: wherefore no regrets. . . . We no longer know what tomorrow may bring. As I indicated, we no longer worry. Only certain is it that the Bosch has started his long way homeward.

To his father he writes on the same day: 'We are now embarked on a very different kind of life; whether one considers it preferable or otherwise to the previous depending on one's moods'. Deprived now of most of his creature comforts, 'bleached with chalk and grown hairy,' he concludes his letter almost exultantly: 'For the present, rain and dirt and damp cold. O for a bath! Much love to all'. Writing to Watts the same day he reminisces in his hungry state on 'the one or two or three outstandingly admirable meals' of his life. It is to Watts, with whom he seems to have the closest emotional tie at this time, that he confesses his fears: 'To be able to prove oneself no coward to oneself, will be great, if it comes off: but suppose one finds oneself fail in the test? I dread my own censorious self in the coming conflict—I also have great physical dread of pain. . . . Pray that I ride my frisky nerves with a cool and steady hand'.

Yet it is clear that Sorley is excited by the turn of events and when his battalion is moved into the front-line trenches north of Loos, he proves himself no coward. The 7th Suffolks took over the trenches after dark on October 12th, having rehearsed before hand all details of the plan to attack two trenches known as the Hairpin south of the Hohenzollern redoubt. Following a preliminary bombardment, the actual attack began at 2 p.m. the next day, when B Company advanced across the open under cover of a smoke screen, whilst A and D Companies attacked the Hairpin itself. But the smoke lifted and B Company were caught in the open by machine-gun fire, suffering heavy casualties. As a result Sorley's D Company and A Company met with heavy opposition and in the confusion Sorley's commander was seriously wounded. Sorley was sent for and took over the Company. Sorley was making sure of the defences against fire from the flank when he was shot in the head by a sniper. His head fell gently forward on the sandbag he had been adjusting and those beside him could scarcely believe he was dead. The manner of his death was in keeping with his unromantic view of life. He was buried next morning near the place he had died. In his kit-bag was found a poem, hastily scribbled in pencil. It is undated, but the contents prove beyond doubt that it was written after the real fighting had started. For what few hopes he had previously felt about death and any curiosity have entirely vanished. Yet even in this bleakest and best of all his war poems there is no more than a passing reference, which is turned into a nightmare image, to the horrifying physical details he must have encountered in the last two weeks of his life. It is Sorley's final answer to Brooke's romantic vision of death and a striking memorial to his own:

When you see millions of the mouthless dead
Across your dreams in pale battalions go,
Say not soft things as other men have said,
That you'll remember. For you need not so.
Give them not praise. For, deaf, how should they know
It is not curses heaped on each gashed head?
Nor tears. Their blind eyes see not your tears flow.
Nor honour. It is easy to be dead.
Say only this, 'They are dead.' Then add thereto,
'Yet many a better one has died before.'
Then, scanning all the o'ercrowded mass, should you
Perceive one face that you loved heretofore,
It is a spook. None wears the face you knew.
Great death has made all his for evermore.*

*For further analysis of this poem see pages 211-13.

10
Conclusion

Sorley's was a brief life and, up to the outbreak of war, an apparently uneventful one. A happy childhood in Scotland was followed by prep. school at Cambridge and a successful public school career at Marlborough. Yet, looking back on his life, there are a number of questions which arise.

The first of these is the question of Sorley's Scottish origins. He certainly had his share of 'canny' good sense, or hard-headedness, if we are to accept this as a racial characteristic. More importantly, however, being a Scot in England seems to have given Sorley a more than usual sense of detachment from his surroundings. And it is this highly objective approach to experience which makes his war poems in particular so powerful. Refusing to be moved by Rupert Brooke's patriotic fervour he sees that:

Victor and vanquished are a-one in death:
Coward and brave: friend, foe. Ghosts do not say
'Come, what was your record when you drew breath?'
But a big blot has hid each yesterday
So poor, so manifestly incomplete.

In keeping with this impartiality, there is a marked absence of gruesome physical details to provoke one to pity for the dead, or anger against the enemy. For the enemy himself is as dear to Sorley as his fellow-soldiers. In a letter to Wynne Willson from Schwerin, only a few months before the outbreak of war, Sorley had confessed that his first feeling of patriotism came to him in Germany, when he heard the soldiers singing 'something glorious and senseless about the Fatherland . . . And when I got home, I felt I was a German, and proud to be a German: when the tempest of the singing was at its loudest, I felt that perhaps I could die for Deutschland—

and I have never had an inkling of that feeling about England, and never shall'. After several months more in Germany he felt a greater affinity with and admiration for the Germans than he did for either the English or the Scots. So that, when war broke out, he was not only immune to the jingoism that surrounded him, but was actively sympathetic towards the enemy, whom he nevertheless believed must be fought. This gives him a unique position among the early war poets and a strong historical importance.

Another fascinating question for the biographer is why Sorley turned to poetry to express himself. None of his immediate family or ancestors wrote poetry, though a number wrote prose. None of his friends chose verse as their medium. In fact, as Sorley himself remarked, writing poetry was looked upon with some suspicion in English public schools. Unlike many young poets, such as Rosenberg and Sassoon, he was not miserable or isolated as a child and thus forced back upon himself. On the contrary he seems to have been in almost every situation happy and well-adjusted. Yet from his earliest years he wrote as though he had no choice. This puzzled and pleased his family, who wanted to publish some of his poems privately in June 1915. But publication does not seem to have been nearly as important to Sorley as the writing itself and he put them off, referring to his own talent as of the 'small-holdings type'. He wrote because he had something he wanted to say, rather than as a self-conscious aesthete, who thought it 'interesting'—a pose which his fellow-schoolboys and soldiers would have discouraged in any case. There are one or two exceptions among his juvenilia, where he seems to be experimenting with verse for verse's sake, but in each case they are inferior productions.

Finally, there is the question of Sorley's twinship. It is tempting to suggest that this endowed him with an almost double consciousness. For one of his most marked features is his highly developed awareness. He was aware, through his own experience, of how it felt to succeed, yet he was also conscious through his twin's sufferings, of the miseries of failure. Indeed, while still at Marlborough he wrote 'A Tale of Two Careers', in which he entered imaginatively into the experience of both the successful and the failures at public school and, in spite of his own undoubted success at Marlborough, he appears to sympathize more with the failures. As I suggested earlier he seems to have felt some guilt at his own effortless superiority to his twin, though this must not be exaggerated.

Whatever the reasons, Sorley was almost invariably sympathetic and thoughtful towards others, especially those less privileged than himself. One small instance of this is his repeated request to his mother from France to send Woodbine cigarettes for his men rather than anything more for himself. Far from taking credit for his generosity and thoughtfulness, he was highly self-critical, suspecting himself of being 'an egoist, sentimentalist or poser'. Gifted as he was, he recognized the dangers of becoming conceited and frequently accused himself of it. He felt that his initial reaction to the outbreak of war had been both 'selfish' and 'subjective', though it would be hard to find a less selfish or more objective one. He was, as he claimed, 'a critic by nature', but in his own case the criticism was seldom justified. For there were few people more modest than Sorley. One manifestation of this was his reluctance to be photographed, which he overcame only when his mother positively demanded it. A more convincing sign of his modesty was his unwillingness to relate anything favourable about himself. It was only through a brother-officer that Sorley's parents learnt of their son's courage and ingenuity during a night-raid on the Germans. Sorley allowed himself only the most indirect reference to the incident, though his quick-wittedness had saved the lives of at least two men:

Hard 'spade-work' (as school reports used to say)—
'curry' in the form of occasional skirmishes at night
between patrols—still keep our days full and our nights
unquiet [he writes to his mother]. Armed with bombs
and equipped with night one can do much raiding
with extraordinary safety . . .

Sorley was far readier to relate stories against himself,
such as the occasion when he told the Beutins he did
not care what he ate and then, when faced with a large
plate of bread, 'quickly recanted and grovelled, sold my
soul for German sausage and climbed down'. For one of
Sorley's most attractive qualities was a strong sense of
humour. This ranged from the facetiousness of some of
his letters to his schoolfriend Alan Hutchinson—'I at last
discovered the Ad. (the syllables jutant are not *ad*ded by
the really smart)'—to the controlled phrasing and timing
of his many witty anecdotes:

Nothing has been happening here [he wrote to his
parents from Jena], except that policemen have been
worrying me. On the memorable date of my entrance
in Jena I had to write two biographies of myself, one
for the university and one for the town. The university
thought that Charles was a masculine, the town that it
was a feminine, name. So when they drew up their
statistics, they didn't tally. So they called on me to-
day and put the whole matter in my hands. I had also
filled up minor details, such as 'faith-confession' and
'since when educated' differently in both. So that
they rather suspected that there were really two of
me and I was keeping one of them beneath the washstand: one of them being a Church of England lady
who had been educated since September 1908, the
other an evangelical gentleman who had begun his
education as early as May 1895.

Sorley had a more serious side to him, as his poems

show. Apart from a little humorous and occasional verse, his poetry deals with important questions, such as the problems of religious faith, the horrors of war and the finality of death. As we have seen, Sorley identified with Goethe's Faust—'er unbefriedigt jeden Augenblick'[1] —in his restless search for truth. Characteristically he preferred spring, autumn and even winter to summer, which seemed to him 'stagnating'. 'There is no more spring (in both senses) anywhere,' he wrote to Arthur Watts from France. 'When the corn is grown and the autumn seed not yet sown, it has only to bask in the sun, to fatten and ripen: a damnable time for men; heaven for the vegetables. And so I am sunk deep in "Denkfaulheit",[2] trying to catch in the distant but incessant upper thunder of the air promise of October rainstorms: long runs clad only in jersey and shorts over the Marlborough downs, cloked in rain, as of yore'. Similarly he preferred unpalatable truths to comfortable illusions. In his honesty he was forced to reject orthodox Christianity, yet his work conveys strong religious beliefs and a mystical sense of rightness in the universe, despite its apparent chaos. Though his early pantheistic beliefs become inadequate in the face of war, he still manages to convey a profound sense of belief in something, if only in his fellow men:

And your bright Promise, withered long and sped,
Is touched, stirs, rises, opens and grows sweet
And blossoms and is you, when you are dead.

However, confronted by the futile carnage of actual warfare in the last months of his life, Sorley's faith appears to waver if not vanish completely, for his final sonnet, 'When You See Millions of the Mouthless Dead' is bereft of any kind of hope.

Yet basically Sorley remains for us a spiritual person

[1]He every moment still unsatisfied.
[2]mental lethagy.

and this spiritual side of his nature seems somewhat at variance with the impression we also have of a healthy, uncomplicated, mischievous schoolboy and popular officer, who ran a pub for his men and supplied them with suet puddings and mouth-organs. There was also a highly sensual side to Sorley, which he first became aware of in the lush valley of northern France, but which had been evident long before in his love of good food and his response to rain on his bare skin, for instance. Paradoxically it is also clear that he was somewhat puritannical, particularly in his suspicion of ease and comfort. These apparent contradictions are, however, an essential part of Sorley's character. He was, even to those closest to him, something of an enigma. His father could not fail to agree with the opinion of an admirer, who wrote to him shortly after Sorley's death: 'His seems to have been a combination of qualities whose like I cannot recall— decision and tenderness, pride and humility, power to feel and to express, the health and strength of the schoolboy and the sensitiveness to beauty of Nature and of words that are too often given only to the recluse'. Indeed at times Sorley appeared something of a recluse, with his love of solitary walks or runs on the downs and his journeys from Cambridge to Marlborough on foot alone. Yet, as his mother points out, there is also something of a paradox, for 'no-one more enjoyed and valued his friends, or more willingly took and gave the best of company'. His letters to Hutchinson, Hopkinson, Harvey, Pelly, Atkey, Gidney and Wynne Willson prove beyond doubt his desire to make and keep friends among boys and masters alike. He could not even enjoy a trip to Schiller's birthplace at Weimar, because he was not in congenial company. Yet the letters and poems suggest a person of unusual depths and reserves.

It is therefore impossible to sum up Sorley's character in a few words or paragraphs. The overriding impression is one of an enthusiast, who entered wholeheartedly into whatever came his way. Gidney said 'He seemed to have some unique privilege of life'. 'Each new experience,' his mother tells us, 'whether game or book or place or human being—came as an adventure to him'. The Master of Marlborough remembered that he was 'never dull or depressed. In fact a bubbling joy in life was one of his greatest charms. He seemed to revel in all its phases'. Reading Sorley's letters, Professor Bethune-Baker, who had known him as a child, recognized behind them a 'rare soul, pure and strong and sweet'. 'It is all so fresh and straight, so convincingly himself,' he wrote to Professor Sorley, 'so attractive and interesting a self: so independent in his outlook, so seeing and thinking in a way of his own. And there's something contagious about it. I feel as if I too must love the rain and the wind on the downs'. Sorley was, as Geoffrey Bickersteth puts it, 'so rich, so extraordinarily lovable and so intensely *alive* that he seems to those of us who did not know him [well] too good to be true. And yet one looks in vain for faults and inconsistencies'. He was indeed a 'rare soul'.

Sorley's paradoxical nature is reflected in his mature poetry. For beneath its apparent simplicity it conceals great complexity of thought and technique. In fact there is a direct correlation between technical simplicity and profundity of thought; the early poems with their complex rhyme schemes, elaborate stanza forms and frequent archaisms are more readily understandable than the later and apparently more simple works. It may be that when Sorley found something really interesting to say he no longer felt the need to complicate the saying of it. What could be more lucid and yet more puzzling than the following:

> All the hills and vales along
> Earth is bursting into song,
> And the singers are the chaps
> Who are going to die perhaps.

O sing, marching men,
Till the valleys ring again.
Give your gladness to earth's keeping,
So be glad, when you are sleeping.

The development of Sorley's poetry from his earliest epic lays in the manner of Scott and Macaulay and his first published work 'The Tempest' at the age of ten, through his Marlborough poems to his war poems is relatively easy to trace. It is, as with many young poets, a process of falling under different influences, learning a little from each in turn, then finally rejecting their models as they find their own voice. Sorley's first Marlborough poems show such diverse influences as Coleridge, Shakespeare, Robert Louis Stevenson, Wordsworth, Kipling, Browning and Tennyson. It was not until he rejected the many in favour of one 'prophet' as he calls him that his poetry makes much impression. Meredith was his first choice in the attempt to free himself from the Tennysonian tradition. Meredith was quickly usurped by Masefield, whose desire to write poetry 'for the people' in simple language that they could understand appealed to Sorley's youthful rebelliousness against the 'establishment' in church, school and society. His allegiance to Masefield either provoked or fitted in with his rejection of such 'aesthetes' as Pater, whose 'fine' writing he despised. Predictably, he preferred austere poets like Hardy and Housman, equating, it seems, sincerity with absence of flourish. This suspicion of ornament is almost certainly related to the puritanism which underlies his character.

Sorley's worship of Masefield was a necessary step in working himself free from the Tennysonian tradition, which persisted well into the twentieth century, and in this he resembles the Georgian poets. It was, however, an unconscious resemblance since he had read only the first volume of *Georgian Poetry*. Though he admired

Abercrombie, de la Mare and Gibson, he was not influenced by them to any extent and even Masefield was
'shunted into a siding' when he left Marlborough. The
works which follow, after a break of eight months in
which he wrote only two poems, are free of any dominat-
ing influence. This is one reason why his war poems are
in most respects his best. They also reflect the greater
maturity he had acquired through being on his own in a
foreign country without the protection of school or
home. Finally, the war which brought with it the even
greater responsibility of being an officer and the daily
possibility of death, wound Sorley up to his highest
pitch. The results are as stark and uncompromising as
the life he was living.

Bearing in mind that these last poems were written
in the trenches, with no chance for revision or polishing,
their technique is remarkable. Of the six poems specifically concerned with war, four are sonnets. As I suggested
earlier, Sorley probably chose this disciplined form in
order to gain the greatest control possible over his highly
emotive subject matter. This is best illustrated by his
last sonnet, 'When You See Millions of the Mouthless
Dead', which is to my mind his finest poem. The sonnet
opens with a striking image, reminiscent of the dis-
integrating faces of Goya's 'black' paintings and the silent
horror of the scene is brought out through the repetition
of soft 'm's, 'l's and 's's contrasted with harsh 'd's.

> When you see millions of the mouthless dead
> Across your dreams in pale battalions go.

'Mouthless' here also implies an inability to speak and
this is backed up by 'deaf' and 'blind' later on, thus
emphasizing the impossibility of communicating with
the dead. The resulting sense of negation is further
emphasized by a long list of actual negatives: 'Say not . . .
need not . . . Give them not . . . It is not . . . Nor tears . . .
Nor honour . . . None wears . . .' Thus the main body

of the poem is shaped quite naturally round a series of negative commands, which are clearly meant to counter-act Rupert Brooke's famous 'Think only this of me':

> Say not soft things as other men have said,
> That you'll remember. For you need not so.
> Give them not praise. For, deaf, how should they know
> It is not curses heaped on each gashed head?
> Nor tears. Their blind eyes see not your tears flow.
> Nor honour. It is easy to be dead.

The potentially emotive material is offset by strictly controlled syntactical patterns based on the repetition of various negatives. In sharp contrast to these negatives is the positive command of the opening line of the sestet, 'Say only this,' which leads us to expect something more hopeful and perhaps closer to Brooke. However, all that the poet will concede is a bleak statement of fact and an even bleaker echo from the *Iliad* to remind us that the dead are not necessarily very noble:

> Say only this, 'They are dead.' Then add thereto,
> 'Yet many a better one has died before.'

The use of direct speech at this point emphasizes the importance of this recognition and in the last four lines Sorley hammers home the unromantic truth he has been forced to accept about death:

> Then scanning all the o'ercrowded mass, should you
> Perceive one face that you loved heretofore,
> It is a spook. None wears the face you knew.
> Great death has made all his for evermore.

The last line is more rhetorical than the rest and slightly at odds with the rather colloquial 'spook' of the line before, but it is in keeping with the gravity of the message. Sorley's personification of the power of death brings to mind the Apocalyptic visions of Revelations. It is, admit-tedly, a flourish, but not one that contradicts the views that precede it, since it emphasizes the levelling process of death. Apart from a few unfortunate archaisms, such as 'heretofore', which would almost certainly have been ironed out in revision, the diction is simple, in keeping with the stark simplicity of the message. The imagery is also fairly straightforward; the use of 'gashed head' and 'pale battalions' reminds us that Sorley is writing his poem in the midst of actual fighting. (The poem was found in his kit after his death.) His restraint, in not giving more gruesome physical details nor making more direct references to the subject of his piece, adds to the dreamlike quality he obviously wishes to convey. At the same time it makes us even more aware of the nightmarish existence he was living in the last few days of his life when even the little sleep he could snatch was invaded by corpses. The use of the word 'spook' in the penultimate line reinforces the sense he gives of being haunted.

There can be no doubt that Sorley had seen through the romantic myth of war, but we can only conjecture what he would have gone on to. He had already rejected the realism Sassoon and Owen were to develop so skilfully and he had only a small share of Rosenberg's vision of the grotesque. There is certainly nothing in the three years' fighting which followed his death to suggest that he would have felt very differently about war had he survived. John Masefield, who believed that Sorley was potentially the greatest poet lost in the war, predicted that he might have become our greatest dramatist since Shakespeare. Yet there is little evidence to support this claim. Sorley attempted drama only once in 'The Other Wise Man', which is in no way outstanding. Admittedly he had the detachment necessary to the great dramatist and was increasingly attracted to Shakespeare and Goethe. Possibly he could have written something akin to Hardy's *The Dynasts* which he greatly admired.

A more fruitful speculation concerns his prose, in particular his letters. There are times when he seems happier in this medium than in poetry, perhaps because it conveys a more rounded picture of his engaging personality. There are passages in his later letters which rise to the heights of poetry, yet have all the expansiveness and detail that prose allows:

> Looking into the future one sees a holocaust somewhere: and at present there is—thank God—enough of 'experience' to keep the wits edged (a callous way of putting it, perhaps). But out in front at night in that no-man's land and long graveyard there is a freedom and a spur. Rustling of the grasses and grave tap-tapping of distant workers: the tension and silence of encounter, when one struggles in the dark for moral victory over the enemy patrol: the wail of the exploded bomb and the animal cries of wounded men. Then death and the horrible thankfulness when one sees that the next man is dead: 'We won't have to *carry* him in under fire, thank God; dragging will do': hauling in of the great resistless body in the dark, the smashed head rattling: the relief, the relief that the thing has ceased to groan: that the bullet or bomb that made the man an animal has now made the animal a corpse. One is hardened by now: purged of all false pity: perhaps more selfish than before. The spiritual and the animal get so much more sharply divided in hours of encounter, taking possession of the body by swift turns.

Sorley undoubtedly had great talent as a prose writer, which developed rapidly in the trenches, where it was probably easier to concentrate on than poetry. It may be that he would have taken it up seriously after the war.

In fact while still at Marlborough Sorley had considered the possibility of journalism as a career, though this was closely bound up with his determination to take up social work of some kind. 'I had always an idea that when you were a fair specimen of the idle rich,' he joked with his friend Hutchinson, 'and I a journalist and socialist orator campaigning against the same at street corners, you would ask me to stay occasionally and give me oysters and champagne'. As we know, Sorley's ambition was not to become a great poet, but a great reformer of the Alexander Paterson type, and he might well have given up writing altogether had he survived the war. As it was he found himself in a curiously fluid situation. In spite of all the petty restrictions of army life it seemed to him freer and more real than the academic life he had reluctantly agreed to follow. For the first time in his somewhat conventional existence, despite the fact that he now faced almost certain death, he felt liberated. And it is from the trenches that he writes his most exultant and positive letter of all to his friend Arthur Watts:

> . . . but where, while riding in your Kentish lanes, are you riding twelve months hence? I am sometimes in Mexico, selling cloth: or in Russia, doing Lord knows what: in Serbia or the Balkans: in England, never. England remains the dream, the background: at once the memory and the ideal. Sorley is the Gaelic for wanderer. I have had a conventional education: Oxford would have corked it. But this has freed the spirit, glory be. Give me *The Odyssey*, and I return the New Testament to store. Physically as well as spiritually, give me the road.
>
> Only sometimes the horrible question of bread and butter shadows the dream: it has shadowed many, I should think. It must be tackled. . . .
>
> Details can wait—perhaps for ever.

Index